MW01204640

Prophetic Destiny

The Saints in the Rocky Mountains

Prophetic Destiny

The Saints in the Rocky Mountains

Paul Thomas Smith

Covenant Communications, Inc.

This book is dedicated to my parents, Joseph T. and Lillian Smith, and to my wife, Gail, and to our nine children and four grandchildren. My parents instilled within me a great love for my heritage and the motivation to preserve it for generations to come. My family has ever been my inspiration, my joy, and my happiness. The Savior's love and teachings dispel the darkness and illuminate my path. For all of this I am eternally grateful.

Published by Covenant Communications, Inc.
American Fork, Utah

Printed in the United States of America
First Printing: May 1996

01 00 99 98 97 96   10 9 8 7 6 5 4 3 2 1

ISBN 1-55503-918-9

Cover Photos: © LDS Church Historical Department Used by permission.

Introduction

Since Joseph Smith's First Vision, revelation and prophecy have been a sustaining force in the lives of the apostles and prophets—gifts of the Spirit that have enabled the Lord's servants to reveal His will to mankind. Dreams and visions were seemingly more prevalent in Joseph Smith's day than ours because in matters of doctrine, organization, and practice, Church leaders had little precedent to follow, save the ancient scriptures. Their need for revelation was often immediate, and that revelation came by obeying the scriptural injunction taught by Jesus: "Ask of God; ask, and it shall be given you; seek, and ye shall find; knock, and it shall be opened unto you. For every one that asketh, receiveth; and he that seeketh, findeth; and unto him that knocketh, it shall be opened" (JST Matthew 7:12-13).

Revelation was not—and is not—confined to Church leaders but can come to any faithful follower of Jesus Christ. In Church history, revelation has clearly come more readily to those who have sacrificed much of their earthly associations and possessions to build the kingdom of God. Thus through the years, countless Latter-day Saints have heeded the Lord, exercised their faith, and have received marvelous manifestations, some of which are recorded, not only within the pages of Church history, but also in personal diaries and journals. Such revelations have come to comfort and strengthen the weary and downcast, to bestow specific blessings, and to reveal in part an individual's potential destiny. However, while revelation may reveal one's mortal and eternal possibilities, it does not replace careful planning, common sense, and hard work to bring those blessings to reality.

Elder John Taylor of the Council of the Twelve served as a missionary to the British Isles during the years 1840-1841. Before he and his companions left Illinois on their mission, they were instructed by the Prophet Joseph Smith to say nothing to new members, for the time being, about "gathering with the Saints" in America. The brethren followed counsel. However, no sooner had converts been baptized than they strongly desired to be with the main body of the Saints in the United States. A number of them dreamt of boarding ships with other Latter-day Saints and sailing to America. "I find it difficult to keep anything from the Saints," wrote Elder Taylor, "for the Spirit of God reveals it to them."[1]

Likewise, in my years of studying Church history, I have found that whenever the Lord prepares to introduce a major change of course for the Saints, a number of the faithful throughout the world will be blessed with prophetic insight about that change as it pertains to their own lives and missions. That knowledge may come through the inspired blessing of a patriarch, in the dreams of the night, through a sudden stroke of inspiration, or, much more rarely, through a divine visitation. However, when such an event occurs, it is not appropriate for that individual to teach as authoritative doctrine what he or she has learned, for *the prophet alone receives revelation and declares the Lord's will in behalf of the entire Church.*

This book recounts many remarkable stories of prophecy and revelation given to the ancient and modern prophets and to individual Saints in preparation for their relocation from the United States to the Rocky Mountains. The number to whom that knowledge was imparted was relatively small, however, until 1842, when the Lord's plan became more commonly known among the people. These stories are a testimony that God rules in the affairs of man and has a guiding hand over the destiny of His people, His church, and His kingdom.

Paul Thomas Smith
A Latter-day Saint in the Rocky Mountains
February 1996

We Came West Willingly—Because We Were Obliged To!

Elder George A. Smith of the Quorum of the Twelve was a veteran pioneer—among the first to enter Great Salt Lake Valley. He was well-known among the Saints, not only for his huge girth and comical hairpiece, but also for his oft-repeated statement about that epic trek: "The Saints willingly came here," he said, "—because they were obliged to!"[2] That statement no doubt brought many smiles and some laughter in every audience. But were the Saints *obliged* to come west? Did they come simply to escape their enemies in Illinois? Elder Smith's brethren of the Twelve knew that coming west was more than a flight from persecution—it was part of the Lord's grand design for His people.

Flights to Freedom in Every Dispensation

In every dispensation of time, the Lord's people have been forced to flee into the wilderness. Adam and Eve left the Garden of Eden and traveled northward to the Valley of Adam-ondi-Ahman (see Moses 4:29-31; D&C 78:15; 107:53-57; 116). Enoch's people were removed from a land and a people of great wickedness and taken into the heavens (see Moses 7:18-21). Noah's family was preserved on the ark from an apostate world (see Moses 7:43; 8:3). The Prophet Jared and his brother Mahonri Moriancumr led their people from the Tower of Babel across countless miles and bodies of water to a "choice land" chosen by the Lord (Ether 1:33-43). Abraham escaped with his family from Ur and a satanic priesthood to Canaan (see Genesis 12:2; 17:6; 18:18; Abraham 1:2, 19); Melchizedek and the city of Salem were taken into heaven (see JST Genesis 14:32-34); Moses led the Israelites from bondage in Egypt (see Exodus 3-14); Lehi and his family fled from certain death in Jerusalem, traveling through a barren wilderness and crossing oceans in an epic trek to a promised land (see 1 Nephi 2:1-2; 20). King Mosiah brought righteous Nephites from the sinful land of Nephi to the land of Zarahemla (see Omni 12–13). The apostle John saw the Christian Church portrayed in vision as a woman in distress: "And the woman fled into the wilderness [the heavens]," John wrote, where she had a place prepared of God" (JST Revelation 12:6).

Thus not only have the Lord's Saints been forced to flee in every dispensation, but in every case the Lord has prepared a promised land for his faithful, covenant people. This has been true even in "secular history": British Puritans and pilgrims helped prepare for the Restoration when they sought religious freedom in America, where they could worship as they pleased (see 1 Nephi 13:13-19). However, for several generations, many Americans were no more tolerant of religious minorities than the Church of England had been. Like their predecessors in other dispensations, members of the Church were forced to flee—in this case from New York to Ohio, and from Missouri and Ohio to Illinois, and from Illinois to Mexican territory.

Preparation Through Prophecy

Almost from the beginning, the Saints anticipated building Zion in Jackson County, Missouri. But the Lord, knowing the Saints would fail in their quest, planned for his people to come west. He gradually prepared his prophets and Church members for that event through prophecy and revelation. In March 1831, the Lord said that before his second coming to the earth, "*Zion* shall flourish upon the hills *and rejoice upon the mountains,* and shall be assembled together unto the place which I have appointed" (D&C 49:24-25, emphasis added). There is no evidence that the Saints comprehended the meaning of the revelation at that time. Years later they came to understand that the Lord prophesied the establishment of the Church upon the hills of midwestern America, as well as the Rocky Mountains, before its return to Jackson County, Missouri.

The West the Saints would come to embrace was known as Upper California, or New Spain, and was Mexican territory. New Spain was home to several thousand Native Americans and temporary home for a handful of American, French, and British trappers and traders—a wild and forbidding place in the minds of many Americans.

Many of the native Americans living in the Rocky Mountains were descendants—in part—of the house of Israel—descendants of Joseph of Egypt through his son Manasseh (see Alma 10:3). Before he died, Jacob (Israel) blessed his son Joseph, prophesying, "Joseph is a fruitful bough, even a fruitful bough by a well; whose branches run over the wall. . . . The blessings of thy father have prevailed above the blessings of my progenitors *unto the utmost bound of the everlasting hills;* they shall be on the head of Joseph, and on the crown of the head of him that was separate from his brethren" (Genesis 49:22, 26).

Years later, Joseph told family members that the Lord Himself had explained the meaning of his blessing: "The Lord hath visited me, and I have obtained a promise of the Lord, that out of the fruit of my loins, the Lord God will raise up a righteous branch . . . *and* [that branch] *shall be carried into a far country;* nevertheless they shall be remembered in the covenants of the Lord . . . [who] shall bring them out of darkness into light; out of hidden darkness, and out of captivity unto freedom" (JST Genesis 50:24-25). The American continent was that "far country." Joseph's "righteous branch," or Father Lehi's family, would one day evolve into the Native Americans, including those living in the "everlasting hills," or Rocky Mountains. Beginning in 1847, that branch of Joseph's family would be joined by another righteous branch—the Latter-day Saints, who came, in part, to "bring [the Lamanites] out of darkness into light; out of hidden darkness, and out of captivity unto freedom" (ibid.).

A Missouri Prophecy

LDS Church Historical Department.

In 1831, the Rocky Mountains were far from the thoughts and plans of Church leaders. As early as April 1829, Joseph Smith was divinely directed to "seek to bring forth and establish the cause of Zion," a charge given four times (D&C 6:6; 11:6; 12:6; 14:6). By September 1830, **Oliver Cowdery** and several companions were directed to preach the gospel to the Lamanites, "and no man knoweth where the city of Zion shall be built, but . . . it shall be on the borders by the Lamanites" (D&C 28:9). The first missionaries made their way to Missouri and vainly sought for permission to teach the gospel to several Native American tribes who had been forcibly relocated onto government lands just west of the Missouri River.

When Joseph Smith visited Independence, Jackson County, in 1831, he received a revelation in which the Lord described that part of Missouri as "the land which I have appointed and consecrated for the gathering of the saints. Wherefore, this is the land of promise, and the place for the city of Zion" (D&C 57:1-2). It was the place designated by the Lord for a sacred city, also known to ancient prophets as "New Jerusalem," where a magnificent complex of temples will bless the formerly "lost" ten tribes, who will gather there to receive the ordinances of exaltation (see, for example, the Lord's prophecy to the Nephites in 3 Nephi 20:22; 21:23-24; see also D&C 42:36; 45:67; 84:3-4; 133:26-35; and many others). Beginning in 1831, hundreds of Saints began settling in Jackson County, Missouri, to help establish Zion.

Although Independence was a wild and uncultured frontier settlement—the "jumping-off place" for travelers headed toward Santa Fe, California, and Oregon—it had a glorious past. In 1857 Brigham Young reminded the Saints, "Now it is a pleasant thing to think of and to know where the Garden of Eden was.

Did you ever think of it? I do not think many do, for in Jackson County was the Garden of Eden. Joseph [Smith] has declared this, and I am as much bound to believe that as to believe that Joseph was a prophet of God."³

Paulina Eliza Phelps

In 1832, Joseph Smith visited Jackson County once again. While there he gathered the Saints' children together in the home of Lyman Wight and blessed them. Five-year-old **Paulina Eliza Phelps** received the Prophet's blessing. She recalled, "In blessing me [Joseph] said that I should live to go to the Rocky Mountains. I did not know at the time what the term 'Rocky Mountains' meant, but I supposed it to  be something connected with the Indians. This frightened me for the reason that I dreaded the very sight of an Indian."⁴

Joseph Holbrook

That December, **Joseph Holbrook** was wrestling with whether or not he should be baptized when he had an apocalyptic experience:

> One night, I dreamed I was in a certain city where people were engaged in their various business matters when all of a sudden a voice was heard from the heavens saying, "Up, get ye out of this city for behold I will  destroy this people, and flee ye into the west." The people all heard the voice and knew it was from heaven. They halted,

looked amazed for a moment and then pursued their course as before. Shortly the voice was heard the second time. The people were seemingly less alarmed than before and again the third time. [The voice] spoke the third time the same words with the same warning, but the people paid no attention to it, so I stopped and marvelled and said "I am not going to stay here" *so I started out of the city to the west.* I found about a dozen more had taken the same warning as myself and we all met at the outside of the city. *We went down a long hill when we came into a large valley running north and south and also a large river running in the midst of the valley running north.* It was both wide and deep and there appeared no way to cross the river. Some said "Let's go up the river" and other said "Let's go down the river," but I said "We were commanded to go to the west. I am going straight into the river." I no sooner got into the river than I found myself on the other bank on the west side and it was said unto me, "You are now baptized." I thought that those who were with me on the other side were with me now, but I did not see how they came.

Now there were three large roads presented before me. One led partly up the river bearing around a hill, one partly down the river bearing around the same hill, while the other went straight forward up the hill, but the hill looked hard to ascend while those wound around to the right and left appeared easy and would finaly [sic] come to the same spot at the top of the hill. The travel in each road was about equal. Those that were with me said, "Let's take the right or left hand road; it will take us much easier to the top of the hill;" but I said *"We are to go straight to the west.* I am going to take the middle road up the hill."

As the several roads were sandy or loamy, I could see the footsteps of men and women and children who had traveled up those roads before me. And as I began to travel up the straight forward road up the hill, it did seem as though the hill became more level, but after traveling on for awhile there was a very bad place in the hill. There were roads that turned off at the foot of this bad hill to the right and left and appeared to wind around the hill and come to the top. The same arguments were used by those that were with me as before "that it would be much easier for [us] to take these winding roads that lead around the hill for what is the use of being so particular which road we travel . . . if we only get to the top of the hill."

I told them I would not turn away from the straight forward road although it did appear that nearly one-half of the people did turn away from the straight forward road. And I did not see them at the top of the hill. Thus I continued my journey finding often a bad hill in the straight forward road while the byroads at the foot of each hill took away much of the travelers and as I came near the end of my journey the obstacles in the road were much more hideous to look at while the byroads look[ed] much more pleasant.

At last I came to the top of the last hill on a level plain. The road had become a small path. I turned around to see what had become of those who had left the straight forward road when it was said to me, "Few there are that will ever come to the top of the hill, few there are that will be saved." I marvelled greatly and thanked the Lord that He preserved me to come to the top of the hill on a level with my brethren while thousands that had set out on the same journey had turned away at the bottom of the hill in those byroads and are lost . . . while the roads became plain before me *that I saw every road that turned away was wrong.* They would fork and those forks would fork again until they ended in total dimness where there is no road. And those travelers often wandering for thousands of years before they could again reach the bottom of the hill and have the privilege of coming up as before. And these that turned away near the top of the hill or near the end of the journey, it took much the longest. I looked to see if my wife was coming, saying, "I think she will be along soon" as she at this time didn't fully believe Mormonism, and I saw the city I had left given over to destruction of every kind by the judgments of God and the wickedness of the people and lo and behold I awoke. It was a dream.[5]

Zion and Zion's Camp

By 1833, the Saints in Jackson County were driven out by enemies of the Church, and most of the Mormons relocated in counties to the north. While the Saints had initially thought of Zion alone as Jackson County, the Mormon newspaper *The Evening and Morning Star* defined Zion as "the section of country from the Mississippi to the Rocky Mountains."[6] The Prophet Joseph also enlarged the concept of geographic Zion when, in 1834, he spoke to the men of Zion's Camp, a hundred men in Kirtland, Ohio, who were organized to bring relief supplies to the Saints in northern Missouri and to assist them in returning to their properties in Jackson County.

Wilford Woodruff remembered Joseph's prophecy given on the night of the departure of Zion's Camp:

> I want to say to you before the Lord [said Joseph] that you know no more concerning the destinies of this Church and Kingdom than a babe upon its mother's lap. You don't comprehend it. It is only a little handful of Priesthood you see here tonight, but this Church will fill North and South America— it will fill the world. It will fill the Rocky Mountains. There will be tens of thousands of Latter-day Saints who will be gathered in the Rocky Mountains, and there they will open the door for the establishing of the Gospel among the Lamanites. . . . This people will go into the Rocky Mountains; they will there build temples to the Most High. They will raise up a posterity there, and the Latter-day Saints who dwell in these mountains will stand in the flesh until the coming of the Son of Man. The Son of Man will come to them while in the Rocky Mountains.[7]

The Blessing of Lorenzo Dow Young

Zion's Camp was unsuccessful in restoring the Saints to their lost lands, but on 22 June 1834, the Lord revealed an extraordinary blessing for those of the camp who remained true and faithful despite the disappointing failure of the expedition. The Lord promised: "Verily I say unto you, it is expedient in me that the first elders of my church should receive their endowment from on high in my house, which I have commanded to be built unto my name in the land of Kirtland" (D&C 105:33).

LDS Church Historical Department.

The commandment to build a **temple in Kirtland** (right) was received in a revelation given over a three-day period (27-28 December 1832 and 3 January 1833; see D&C 88:119 ff.). As the temple neared completion, 28-year-old **Lorenzo Dow Young** (below), the youngest of John Young's five sons, was assigned to plaster the exterior and score the plaster so it would appear as brick. Exposure to the elements made Lorenzo vulnerable to illness; by early 1836 he hovered near death in Kirtland, Ohio, from consumption (most likely tuberculosis, complicated by a severe case of pneumonia), and was unable to talk. Dr. Frederick G. Williams and a Dr. Seely

LDS Church Historical Department.

carefully examined Lorenzo and told John Young that his son's lungs were essentially destroyed from the disease. "Mr. Young," said Dr. Seely, "unless the Lord makes your son a new pair of lungs, there is no hope for him!"

John Young hurried to the Prophet Joseph and said, "Lorenzo is dying; can there not be something done for him?" The Prophet thought for a moment and said "Yes! Of necessity, I must go away to fill an appointment which I cannot put off. But you go and get my brother Hyrum, and, with him, get together twelve or fifteen good faithful brethren; go to the house of Brother Lorenzo, and all join in prayer. . . . Let [them] anoint Brother Young with oil; then lay hands on him [and bless him] until you receive a testimony that he will be restored."

John Young strictly followed Joseph's instructions, and Lorenzo received several blessings from the brethren. Lorenzo recalled that when Hyrum Smith laid his hands on his head, "the Spirit rested mightily upon him. He was full of blessing and prophecy . . . he said that I should live to go with the Saints into the bosom of the Rocky Mountains, to build up a place there. . . ."

"At that time," wrote Lorenzo, "I had not heard about the Saints going to the Rocky Mountains. . . . After [Hyrum] had finished he seemed surprised at some things he had said, and wondered at the manifestations of the Spirit. I coughed no more . . . and rapidly recovered."[8] Lorenzo was completely healed. He outlived all of his brothers, including Brigham, and died in Salt Lake City in 1895 at the age of eighty-eight.

The day Joseph Smith met Brigham Young for the first time, he afterward remarked that the time would come when Elder Young would preside over the Church. Four years later, the Prophet Joseph received a manifestation that affirmed that Brigham Young would play an important role in bringing the gospel to the Lamanites in the West. On the evening of 21 January 1836, Joseph Smith witnessed several visions of great significance in the attic story of the Kirtland Temple. "I saw Elder Brigham Young standing in a strange land," said Joseph, "in the far south and west, in a desert place, upon a rock in the midst of about a dozen men of color [Native Americans], who appeared hostile. He was preaching to them in their own tongue, [with] the angel of God standing above his head, with a drawn sword in his hand, protecting him, but he did not see it."[9]

A Blessing Given To Erastus Snow

Brigham Young was not the only Church leader to be designated by revelation for preaching the gospel in the West. **Erastus Snow**, a relative of Lorenzo Snow, was given a blessing in Kirtland," predicting that he should yet be employed in the ministry west of the Rocky Mountains, and should there perform a good work in teaching and leading the Lamanites west of the Rocky Mountains."[10] Erastus would

later be ordained an apostle and serve among the Native Americans in southern Utah.

On 23 July 1837, the Prophet Joseph Smith received a revelation in behalf of Thomas B. Marsh, the first President of the Council of the Twelve in the Restored Church. In describing President Marsh's responsibilities, the Lord said, in part, "Let thy feet be shod also, for thou art chosen, *and thy path lieth among the mountains,* and among many nations." (D&C 112:7) Tragically, Elder Marsh apostatized within a year, so his successor, Brigham Young, fell heir to this prophetic instruction.

The Saints Will Travel East, North, West, and East!

About two years later, **Brigham Young** was living on a farm in northern Missouri, during a brief period when the saints were at peace with their non-Mormon neighbors. During that time he had a revelatory experience about the West which he first publicly related in a sermon in 1856. "It was in the Spring of 1838," Brigham recalled, "before there was any disturbance in . . .

Daviess County. This people, thought I, are obnoxious to these Missourians. Our religion they hate, our Prophet they despise and would like to kill him. They are ignorant of the things of God. . . . Therefore I saw, upon natural principles, that we would be driven from there, but when, I did not know. But still it was plain to me that we would have to leave the State, and that when we *did* leave it we would not go south, north or west, but east, back to the other States. . . . I then saw that we would go north, as a Church and people, and *then* to the West, and that when [the Saints] went to Jackson County, they would go from the west to the east. Mark my words, write them down, this people, as a Church and kingdom, will go from the west to the east."[11]

By August of 1838, the "Mormon War" had broken out, with mobs and Missouri militia members alike pitted against the Saints. During this time of great trial, Joseph apparently began thinking that the Saints ought to flee to the West. Luman Andros Shurtliff, a Latter-day Saint, was living in Missouri at the time. Years later he wrote, "We got into the Salt Lake Valley, September 23, 1851, thankful to the God of Heaven that I and my family were in the valley of the Rocky Mountains—here where the Prophet Joseph Smith had said thirteen years before [in 1838] that the Saints would go if the government did not put a stop to the mobbing and the persecution of them."[12]

Late in November, Joseph Smith and five brethren were imprisoned in Liberty Jail, accused with several very serious but trumped-up charges. Beginning in January of 1839, without their leader, the Saints were forced to flee from Missouri. As Brigham Young had envisioned, they were unable to return south to their former homes, farms, and businesses in Jackson County, for they would be in the midst of their enemies. They could not settle directly to the west, for that was Indian territory, and settlement by whites was forbidden by the United States government. They could travel north into Iowa, which had an abundance of fertile soil, but Iowa lacked a strong enough economic base to support the large Mormon population. The Saints' only option was to travel directly east and cross the Mississippi River into Quincy, Illinois. Some time later, to the north, a swampy and somewhat desolate site was purchased as a new location for the Saints, because the land was available for a good price. Over the next few years, the Saints transformed their settlement into a near-paradise. Although most Saints did not know it, Nauvoo was only a temporary gathering place for the Saints to regroup. In May of 1839 Heber C. Kimball prophesied that it was "not a long abiding place for the Saints."[13]

Oliver B. Huntington recalled, "When we first went to Nauvoo the old patriarch Joseph (Sr.) came into our house one day and in a very confidential way, giving us to understand that it was not to be made public, asked a question as to how long we thought the Church would stay in Nauvoo, and went on to say that the Lord had told Joseph the Prophet, that we would stay there just seven years, and that when we left there, we would go right into the midst of the Indians, in the Rocky Mountains, as this country, Utah, was then called. This we have seen fulfilled."[14]

Daughters of Utah Pioneers Photo File.

"A Place of Safety"

In 1840, Jonathan Dunham and several other brethren were assigned to teach the gospel to Lamanites living in the eastern United States. While visiting in Kirtland, Dunham told the Saints, "A new scene of things [is] about to transpire in the West, in fulfillment of prophecy." After arriving in Kirtland, Jonathan explained, "This nation is about to be destroyed, but there is a place of safety preparing for [the Saints] away towards the Rocky Mountains . . . but few [Saints] will be preserved to arrive."[15] Elder Dunham was undoubtedly referring to the Prophet Joseph's prophecy of the impending Civil War. Where and when he heard of the Saints fleeing to the West is unknown.

A Dream and a Prophecy

LDS Church Historical Department.

In July 1841, **Wilford Woodruff** spent a few days in Boston while returning to Nauvoo from a mission in England. On the evening of 6 July "he dreamed that the Saints migrated to the Rocky Mountains."[16]

A year later, in August 1842, Joseph Smith was in Montrose, Iowa, to dedicate the "Rising Sun" Masonic lodge. Thomas Bullock recorded Joseph as saying, "I prophesied that the Saints would continue to suffer much affliction and would be driven to the Rocky Mountains. Many would apostatize; others would be put to death by our persecutors or lose their lives in consequence of exposure or disease, and some of you will live to go and assist in making settlements, and build cities, and see the Saints become a mighty people, in the midst of the Rocky Mountains."[17]

Anson Call was present when Joseph's prophecy was given and wrote:

> I had before seen him in a vision and now saw while he was talking his countenance change to white; not the deadly white of a bloodless face, but a living, brilliant white. He seemed absorbed in gazing at something at a great distance, and said: "I am gazing upon the valleys of those mountains. . . . Oh the beauty of those snow-capped mountains! The cool refreshing streams that are running down through those mountain gorges!" Then, gazing in another direction, as if there was a change in locality [Joseph said], "Oh the scenes that this people will pass through! The dead that will lie between here and there!"

Then turning in another direction as if the scene had again changed [Joseph said,] "Oh the apostasy that will take place before my brethren reach that land! But the priesthood shall prevail over all its enemies, triumph over the devil and be established upon the earth, never more to be thrown down!" He then charged us with great force and power, to be faithful in those things that had been and should be committed to our charge, with the promise of all the blessings that the priesthood could bestow."

Anson concluded, "It is *impossible* to represent in words the grandeur of Joseph's appearance, his beautiful descriptions of this land, and his wonderful prophetic utterances as they emanated from that glorious inspirations that overshadowed him. There was a force and power in his exclamations. . . ."[18] Fifty-two years later, on Joseph Smith's eighty-ninth birthday anniversary, Elder Claudius V. Spencer said, "I am a living witness that Joseph predicted in Nauvoo—'My people shall become a numerous and a mighty host in the vastnesses of the Rocky Mountains.' When those words were spoken they would have tested the credulity of any man of the world, as there was not the least likelihood of their fulfillment at that time."[19]

There may not have been "the least likelihood of their fulfillment" at that time, but Brigham Young recalled, "In the days of Joseph we sat many hours at a time conversing about this very country. Joseph often said, 'If I were only in the Rocky Mountains with a hundred faithful men, I would then be happy, and ask no odds of mobocrats.'"[20] But discussions about coming west were not kept between Joseph and Brigham alone; a council was organized to deliberate on various locations for the Saints to gather.

The Oregon and California Expedition

According to Orson Pratt, while the Prophet Joseph was living in Missouri, "he had [a] move [west] in contemplation and always said that we would send a company of young men to explore the country and return before the families can go over the mountains." Then Orson quoted Joseph as saying, "It is decidedly in my mind to do so."[21] Lyman Wight said that such an expedition was a topic of conversation while the Prophet was imprisoned in Liberty Jail.[22]

On 20 February 1844 the Prophet Joseph announced plans to organize twenty-five men into the Oregon and California Expedition to "select a site for a new city for the Saints" in the West. He wrote:

> I instructed the Twelve Apostles to send out a delegation and investigate the location of California and Oregon [Utah was then part of Upper California], and hunt out a good location, where we can be removed to after the temple is completed, and where we can build a city in a day, and have a government of our own, get up into the mountains, where the devil cannot dig us out, and live in a healthful climate, where we can live as old as we have a mind to."[23]

> Send twenty-five men, let them preach the gospel wherever they go. Let that man go that can raise $500, a good horse and mule, a double-barrel gun, one-barrel rifle, and the other smooth bore, a saddle and bridle, a pair of revolving pistols, bowie-knife, and a good sabre. Appoint a leader and let them beat up for volunteers. . . .

Within a week over twenty men had volunteered.[24]

"Joseph, the Prophet, said we would come to the Rocky Mountains," wrote **Bathsheba W. Smith,** "and he had a company of young men selected to hunt a location for a home for the

Saints. Samuel Richards was one of that company. I heard of it while we were in Illinois, and I remember an old lady coming in and talking to Mother about what Joseph, the Prophet, had said. I said I would like the time to come soon, I would like to get away from our enemies. She gave me a right good scolding, saying it was terrible to think of going to the Rocky Mountains."[25]

Samuel Whitney Richards, a twenty-year-old, attended several recruiting sessions for the exploration company, but remained unconvinced that he should become involved. He prayed about the matter and received a startling answer through an extraordinary dream. He later said:

Daughters of Utah Pioneers Photo File.

> I attended four meetings of this company and at one of them, which was in charge of Hyrum Smith, and three or four of the Twelve was also present, it was said that Joseph the Prophet had remarked that he wanted young men for that mission who could go upon the mountains and talk with God face to face, as Moses did upon Mount Sinai. When I heard that statement, I felt in my sour that I was not one to go; and just before the meeting closed I got up out of my seat for the purpose of going to Brother Hyrum Smith and telling him I was not the one to go, for I did not feel that I could meet the conditions, but as I got up there was a voice came to me, and I heard it distinctly as from one standing by my side, saying, "Stop: rest awhile."
>
> I took my seat again, and instead of telling the Prophet Hyrum that I did not feel I could go, I went home, and before retiring I knelt by my bedside and prayed to my heavenly Father. If I ever prayed in earnest, it was then, that I might know before morning whether I was a suitable one to go on that expedition, under the terms specified. The idea of going into the mountains and talking with God face to face, as

Moses did upon Mount Sinai, was more than I, as a boy, could think of encountering. No one perhaps need wonder that I should shrink from such a consideration.

I retired to my bed and remained there about four hours, and during that four hours I got the answer to my prayer, and when I awoke I was prepared to go upon that journey and do just as the Prophet wanted me to do. *During that four hours I saw all that I expect to see if I should live a thousand years.* Someone came to me and told me where to go, and I performed that journey that night while I lay upon my bed. *I came to this* [Salt Lake] *valley first,* I don't know how I got here, but I went down through these valleys and into Southern California. It had been stated that possibly we might have to go that far.

When I came here I had to pass four sentinels, and in passing them I gave a countersign, which I got direct from heaven at the time it was needed. I passed them all, and went on down into Southern California. Then I was prompted to go farther, and I went into the northern part of Mexico. I returned from there to Jackson County, Missouri, and there I stayed and helped build the temple. I saw that temple thoroughly completed; in fact, I labored upon it until it was completed. When this was done, the vision continued, and I went and laid down my body in the ground, and my spirit left this tabernacle. Then I traversed this continent from end to end. *I saw the Garden of Eden as it was in the beginning and as it will be restored again.* It was a land filled with verdure and vegetation, and with all manner of fruits, on which man was living. I saw it filled with cities, towns and villages, and people happy, living under the administration of divine providence. It was a Garden of Eden in very deed.

Now, all this I saw while I was sleeping, and it was so impressed upon me that it can never be forgotten. *I saw that this was the result of the Latter-day Saints coming to these valleys of the mountains and following the direction that the Prophet*

Joseph indicated. . . . I wish to make the statement distinctly, that this coming to the mountains of the Saints of God and establishing themselves here was under the special direction of the Prophet Joseph Smith."[26]

Route of Travel Revealed by the Prophet

Not only did Joseph Smith conclude that the Rocky Mountains would be the future home of the Saints, but he had evidently seen in vision the exact route the pioneers would follow in getting there. At least four brethren testified that that was the case. **Mosiah Hancock** wrote, "The Prophet [Joseph] came to our home and stopped in our carpenter shop and stood by the turning lathe. I went and got my map for him. 'Now,'

he said, 'I will show you the travels of this people.' He then showed our travels through Iowa, and said, 'Here you will make a place for the winter; and here you will travel west until you come to the valley of the Great Salt Lake! You will build cities to the North and to the South, and to the East and to the West; and you will become a great and wealthy people in that land.'[27]

Stephen H. Goddard recalled being in the Nauvoo Masonic Hall when Joseph Smith took a piece of chalk and sketched on the floor the route the Saints would take across the continent until they reached the Great Basin.[28] In 1897 Oliver B. Huntington met Hopkins C. Pender in Salt Lake's Hall of Relics. Oliver recorded that "from him [I] learned that Joseph Smith just before he was killed, made a sketch of the future home of the Saints in the Rocky Mts., and their route or road to that country as he had seen in vision; a map or drawing of it. Levi W. Hancock drew a copy of that map, which copy H. C. Pender had seen. He said that Levi W. Hancock told him that there was 4 copies of that map taken one of which Brigham Young kept, one was carried by the Mormon Battalion by which they knew where to find the church, or Salt Lake Valley."[29]

Years later in St. George, "Father" McBride told the Saints that "Joseph marked with his cane in the sand the track the saints would take to the Rocky Mountains. . . . Said we should travel on thro[sic] the mountains; described the Valley of Great Salt Lake just as tho he had lived there."[30]

However accurate the memories of these brethren, Joseph prophesied that "within five years we should be out of the power of our old enemies, whether they were apostates or of the world. Record what I have said, that when it comes to pass, they need not say they had forgotten the saying."[31]

The Martyrdom

Joseph had known since March 1829 that he would probably die by the hands of assassins. The Lord had exhorted Joseph to "be firm in keeping the commandments wherewith I have commanded you; and if you do this, behold I grant unto you eternal life, *even if you should be slain*" (D&C 5:22, emphasis added). By 1844 Joseph knew it was only a matter of a short time before his death. While visiting with his friend Benjamin Johnson, Benjamin recalled:

> [Joseph] sank down heavily in his chair, and said, "I am getting tired and would like to go to my rest." His words and tone thrilled and shocked me, and like an arrow pierced my hopes that he would long remain with us, and I said, as with a heart full of tears, "Oh! Joseph, what could we, as a people do without you? And what would become of the great Latter-day work if you should leave us?". . . . In reply he said, "Benjamin, I should not be far away from you, and if on the other side of the veil I should still be working with you, and with a power greatly increased, to roll on this kingdom."[32]

A short time later, Joseph and his brother Hyrum lay dead from the gunshot wounds of an assassin. Returning from St. Louis, Missouri, **William C. Staines** saw the bodies of Joseph and Hyrum lying in state in the Mansion House. He said:

Utah State Historical Society.

> I have seen England mourning for two kings and for the husband of her queen, when every shop in London was closed, when every church bell tolled, when every man who drove a cab or conveyance of any kind had a piece of crape tied to the hand of his whip. . . . I have seen this nation mourn for its chief magistrate—President Lincoln. But the scene at Nauvoo was far more affecting. The grief and the sorrow of the LDS people was heartfelt. It was the mourning of a community of many thousands, all of whom revered these martyred brethren as their fathers and benefactors, and the sight of their bleeding bodies—for their blood had not ceased to flow as they lay in their coffins—was a sight never to be forgotten. The mourning I witnessed for king and for our nation's chief was only here and there manifested by tears, but for two who suffered for their religion and their friends, the whole people wept in going to and from the scene—all, all were weeping.[33]

Contenders for the Priesthood Keys

After the martyrdom of the Prophet, some questioned whether priesthood authority remained on the earth. "President Brigham Young told a dream he had concerning a man child whom some say was dead," wrote Allen Stout, "but he looked at him and saw that he breathed, and the child grew fast. 'Now this,' he said, 'was the priesthood; though the Prophet was slain, yet the priesthood remained unhurt.'"[34]

Indeed the priesthood *was* unhurt, and as the president of the Quorum of the Twelve, Brigham Young was the man who had been appointed by the Prophet Joseph, before his death, to preside over the kingdom of God. Mariah Pulsipher wrote, "The mobocrats were continually seeking Joseph's life. He and Hyrum were finally slain. What a time of trouble. . . . That fall . . . I prayed . . . thinking of the situation of the Church, having to leave in the spring. I was not asleep. The room shone bright. . . . A voice spoke, 'I am your ministering spirit.' I asked if Joseph Smith died a true prophet. He spoke, 'He died a true prophet; Brigham Young is now the man to lead the Church."[35]

LDS Church Historical Department.

Mariah Pulsipher's ministering spirit spoke the truth. At the time of the assassinations of Joseph and Hyrum, all of the Twelve save John Taylor and Willard Richards were in the East, campaigning for Joseph Smith's candidacy for president of the United States. Upon learning of their deaths, the brethren returned to Nauvoo as rapidly as possible. **Parley P. Pratt** was in the forefront of the Twelve as he made his way back to Nauvoo in July 1844. He described his experience:

As I walked along over the plains of Illinois, lonely and solitary, I reflected as follows: I am now drawing near to the beloved city; in a day or two I shall be there. How shall I meet the sorrowing widows and orphans? How shall I meet the aged and widowed mother of these two martyrs? How shall I meet an entire community bowed down with grief and sorrow unutterable? What shall I say? Or how console and advise twenty-five thousand people who will throng about me in tears, and in the absence of my President and the older members of the now presiding council, will ask counsel at my hands? Shall I tell them to fly to the wilderness and deserts? Or, shall I tell them to stay at home and take care of themselves, and continue to build the Temple? With these reflections and inquiries, I walked onward, weighed down as it were unto death. When I could endure it no longer, I cried out aloud, saying: "O Lord! In the name of Jesus Christ I pray Thee, show me what these things mean, and what I shall say to Thy people?"

On a sudden the Spirit of God came upon me, and filled my heart with joy and gladness indescribable; and . . . the spirit of revelation glowed in my bosom with as visible a warmth and gladness as if it were fire. The Spirit said unto me: "Lift up your head and rejoice; for behold! *It is well with my servants Joseph and Hyrum. My servant Joseph still holds the keys of my kingdom in this dispensation,* and he shall stand in due time on the earth, in the flesh, and fulfil that to which he is appointed. Go and say unto my people in Nauvoo, that they shall continue to pursue their daily duties and take care of themselves, *and make no movement in Church government to reorganize or alter anything until the return of the remainder of the Quorum of the Twelve.* But exhort them that they continue to build the House of the Lord which I have commanded them to build in Nauvoo."[36]

Parley returned to Nauvoo on July 10. He found that the Lord's counsel was well advised, for Sidney Rigdon had returned from his self-imposed exile in Pittsburgh, Pennsylvania, to claim guardianship for the Church. Parley, Willard Richards, and John Taylor managed to stall any actions on Sidney's part until the arrival of the entire Quorum of the Twelve.

On August 8, a public meeting was convened in a grove so that Sidney and Brigham Young, representing the Twelve, could present their claims for leadership before the Saints. Sidney, the first to speak, argued that he was the only surviving member of the First Presidency, and that eleven years earlier he had been appointed by the Lord as Joseph's spokesman (see D&C 100:9-11); thus he was qualified to serve as the "Guardian of the Church." That afternoon, Brigham Young testified that Sidney's calling ceased with Joseph's death and that Joseph had bestowed all priesthood keys upon the Twelve prior to his assassination.

For a brief time as Brigham spoke, he was transfigured before the eyes and ears of countless Latter-day Saints. Helen Mar Whitney recalled:

> I can bear witness, with hundreds of others who stood that day under the sound of Brigham's voice, of the wonderful and startling effect that it had upon us. If Joseph had risen from the dead and stood before them, it could hardly have made a deeper or more lasting impression. It was the very voice of Joseph himself. This was repeatedly spoken of by the Latter-day Saints. And surely it was a most powerful and convincing testimony to them that he was the man, instead of Sidney Rigdon, that was destined to become the "great leader" and upon whose shoulders the mantle of Joseph Smith had fallen.[37]

Postmortal Appearances of the Prophet Joseph

Four months after his assassination, Joseph reaffirmed the passing of the priesthood keys in a dream witnessed by Wilford Woodruff. Elder Woodruff, who was in Maine preaching the gospel, wrote:

> While I was at the home of my father-in-law I had a peculiar dream. . . . Among other things I was called with the Twelve to hold the keys of the Kingdom in all the world. I traveled with them over much of the earth and I also traveled through many countries alone. When I finished my journey I saw many things which I cannot write, but in the end, Joseph, the Prophet, assisted me to come where he was and pointed out to me my place and work. I immediately entered into the

duties of the new calling to which I was appointed.

The same night I had another dream. I was in the presence of the Prophet, and was conversing with him about his death. I told him I felt bad over it, and that had I known he would have been taken so soon I should have conversed with him more while he lived. I would have asked him many questions. In reply he said that it was not his fault that I did not.[38]

By December Wilford was en route to England to preside over his last mission in that land. Traveling with Elder Woodruff were four brethren and three sisters. He wrote:

We had been traveling three days and nights in a heavy gale and were being driven backwards. Finally I asked my companions to come into the cabin with me, and I told them to pray that the Lord would change the wind. I had no fears of being lost, but I did not like the idea of being driven back to New York, as I wanted to go on my journey. We all offered the same prayer, both men and women; and when we got through we stepped on to the deck and in less than a minute it was as though a man had taken a sword and cut that gale through, and you might have thrown a muslin handkerchief out and it would not have moved it.

The night following this Joseph and Hyrum visited me, and the Prophet laid before me a great many things. Among other things, he told me to get the Spirit of God; that all of us needed it. He also told me what the Twelve Apostles would be called to go through on the earth before the coming of the Son of Man, and what the reward of their labors would be; but all that was taken from me, for some reason. Nevertheless I know it was most glorious, although much would be required at our hands.[39]

William Wines Phelps

LDS Church Historical Department.

Although he was dead, the Prophet's presence and influence remained among the people. As **Joseph F. Smith** (left) said in 1894, "Many have seen the Prophet in vision since his martyrdom, and many more will yet see him in vision."[40] **Elder William W. Phelps** (below) saw the Prophet in a dream the second night after the Prophet's death. William said that Joseph "looked as natural as life, and bore the same self-commanding look. Elder Phelps thought the kingdom appeared to be on wheels, and Joseph asked him why he did not speak to the drivers and have them go ahead with it. Elder Phelps asked Joseph if the kingdom was on wheels, and he said "yes," and told him to drive ahead. Elder Phelps then spoke to the drivers and they drove ahead. He saw the kingdom move around the Temple. Joseph spoke to William as they came round and said, "'you see it moves and receives no harm. Now drive across the river into Iowa."[41]

LDS Church Historical Department.

Anson Call

Anson Call (see photo, opposite page) was deeply distressed at Joseph's death. He wrote:

> The bodies of Joseph and Hyrum were taken to Joseph's mansion and were exhibited to all who wished to see them. I accordingly took my family and took a view of the bodies of the Prophet and Patriarch and returned home with my family.

Sleep and the desire of food had left my body. I shall not attempt to describe my feelings. What was to be done, I knew not. I cried mightily unto the Lord that I might know what to do.

The third night I had a dream, or a vision. . . . I was traveling by myself in a lonely place till I came to a new field about three acres in size. I discovered in the centre [sic] of the field a nice block house. I went to the door of the house. I discovered Joseph standing in the middle of the floor. I sprang and clinched him by the hand. I threw my arms around him, and kissed him, and said, "Joseph, I thought you was dead!" He said, "I am." I said, "This is certainly Joseph." He said, "Yes, this is Joseph; take your seat and I will tell you all about it."

I seated myself and then discovered I was in a congregation of Saints whom I was acquainted with. Joseph then said, "Brethren, I have been killed in Carthage Jail, and it will not make any difference with you, if you will do as you are told. I shall continue to govern and control this kingdom as I have hitherto done. The keys of this kingdom were committed to me. I hold them and shall continue to hold them, worlds without end. I am dead, and I am out of the power of my enemies. I am now where I can do you good. Be no longer troubled. Be faithful, be diligent, do as you are told, and you shall see the salvation of God."

I then discovered myself sitting in bed. I . . . commenced comforting my brethren and told them what I had seen and heard.[42]

Eliza Roxcy Snow Smith

LDS Church Historical Department.

Eliza Roxcy Snow Smith, nearly prostrate with grief at the passing of Joseph, pled with the Lord that she might be permitted to be taken from a wicked world to join her husband. Joseph came to Eliza and told her that she "must not continue to supplicate the Lord in that way, for her petition was not in accordance with His design concerning her." Eliza's work was not yet completed; the Lord and her husband wanted her "to live many years and assist in carrying on the great Latter-day work which Joseph had been chosen to establish; that she must be of good courage and help to cheer, and lighten the burdens of others."[43]

Diantha Farr Clayton

Slightly a year after Joseph's passing, **Diantha Farr Clayton**, a plural wife of William Clayton, was suffering greatly, apparently possessed by an evil spirit. William wrote:

Daughters of Utah Pioneers Photo File.

> I saw that her mind was affected and she was likely to have another fit of mental derangement. Soon as she got laid down she began to toss about and rave as if in great pain which seemed to increase until she was perfectly out of her mind and raging. . . . Brother Farr came down and laid hands on her and rebuked the evil spirit and commanded it to leave her in the name of the Lord. She immediately calmed down and seemed to fall into a mild sleep.

Soon after she commenced talking or rather answering questions. She seemed to be in the world of spirits on a visit, and about the first she conversed with was Brother Joseph and the conversation seemed to be on the subject of the massacre. She then appeared to go and visit a number of dead relatives who invariably enquired about their relatives on earth. The answers she gave were literally facts as they exist. . . . She then appeared to go back to Brother Joseph and Hyrum Smith and Father Smith. Joseph asked about Emma and the children and how the Twelve and Emma felt towards each other and so forth, all which she answered wisely but truly. . . . He asked about me [William Clayton] and told her I was a good man. When she parted with her friends she always bid them "good bye" but when she parted with Joseph she said, "I am not in the habit of kissing men but I want to kiss you" which she appeared to do and then said "farewell." She then seemed to start back for home. She appeared all the time in a hurry to get back. She said she would like to tarry but she could not leave father and mother and another, but she would soon return and bring them with her and then she would tarry with them. She conversed about two hours in this manner and seemed over-joyed all the time. A pleasant smile on her countenance which continued after she awoke. It was one of the most interesting and sweet interviews I ever witnessed, and a very good spirit seemed to prevail all the time. I left about 1 oclock [with her] apparently much composed and comparatively free from pain.[44]

Joseph's Labors in the Spirit World

On 19 August 1844, Wilford Woodruff met in council in Nauvoo with some visiting brethren. Wilford told of a recent dream in which he symbolically witnessed the Prophet Joseph leave the earth to continue his labors in the spirit world: "I met with Br Joseph Smith in the Congregation of the Saints. He had his old Hebrew and Jerman [sic] Bible, and preached to the Saints. B[ut] he seemed to be to[o] thronged by the people and he rose up lifted up a curtain and passed into another room where the people could not distirb [sic] him and there he was going to teach the people."[45]

The Will of the Lord: Finish the Temple!

Although there was peace in Nauvoo for a time following the Prophet's martyrdom, it became increasingly clear to Brigham Young that the Nauvoo Temple needed to be rapidly completed, and immediate preparations undertaken to move the Saints westward. The temple was only a story high. As President of the Twelve, Brigham Young now presided over the Church. On 24 January 1845, he prayed for direction. Brigham wrote, "I inquired of the Lord whether we should stay here and finish the Temple. The answer was we should."[46] The temple soon rose skyward.

Daughters of Utah Pioneers Photo File.

Brigham Young knew that once the temple was complete, the Twelve were to prepare the Saints to move West. One day, **Stephen Martindale Farnsworth**, a temple laborer, had an extraordinary open vision in which he learned this important concept:

As I was going from my house to work on the Temple on a sudden the heavens assumed a hazy and gloomy appearance, and the saints in Nauvoo appeared to be all in confusion and troubled and downcast in countenance, and the Twelve Apostles commenced counseling the Saints to gather in from the various Settlements, and prepare for a great Journey to the West, whereupon the saints gathered themselves together and started on their journey westward in [sic] waggons; in appearance as far as the eye could reach. After traveling some time, the journey seemed to be accomplished much easier than was anticipated and matters seemed to assume a brighter and more chereful apperance [sic] and prosperity attended the saints for a short season."[47]

Once the attic story of the temple was complete, Brigham Young spent the months of December 1845 and January 1846 assisting over five thousand Saints in receiving their endowments. The Saints were preparing to establish Zion in the wilderness, and the Lord wanted them to be under covenants that would enable them to become a Zion people. In January Brigham wrote in his journal: "Such has been the anxiety manifested by the Saints to receive the ordinances, and such was the anxiety on our part to administer to them, that I have given myself up entirely to the work of the Lord in the Temple night and day, not taking more than four hours' sleep, upon an average, per day, and going home but once a week."[48]

During this period of great temple activity, Brigham Young wrote in his journal:

This morning [2 January 1846] Elder Heber C. Kimball related the following dream: Last evening, before retiring to bed he asked God to enlighten his mind with regard to the work of endowment; while sleeping he beheld a large field of corn that was fully ripe, he and a number of others were commanded to take baskets and pick off the corn with all possible speed, for there would soon be a storm that would hinder the gathering of the harvest. The hands engaged in gathering the harvest, were heedless and unconcerned and did not haste, as they were commanded; but he and the man he assisted had a much larger basket than the rest, and picked with all their might of the largest ears of the field, they once in a while would pick an ear that had a long tail on each end and but a few grains scattering over the center of the cob, which were very light.[49]

Brigham Young then explained, "The interpretation of the dream is, that the field represented the Church, the good corn represented good saints, the light corn represented the light and indifferent saints, the laborers are those appointed to officiate in the Temple, *the storm is trouble that is near upon us, and requires an immediate united exertion of all engaged in giving the endowments to the saints, or else we will not get through before we will be obliged to flee for our lives.*[50]

LDS Church Historical Department.

Church leaders understood that temple building and temple work would continue to be a major focus of the Church in their future location. **John D. Lee** reported that in a council meeting, "President Young said that the sayings of the Prophets would never be verified unless the House of the Lord be reared in the Tops of the Mountains and the Proud Banner of Liberty wave over the valleys that are within the Mountains."[51]

Without doubt, Brother Brigham was certainly familiar with Isaiah's prophecy that a temple of great importance would be constructed just prior to the Millennia era. Isaiah wrote, "And it shall come to pass in the last days, that the mountain of the Lord's house shall be established in the top of the mountains, and shall be exalted above the hills, and all nations shall flow unto it. And many people shall go and say, Come ye, and let us go up to the mountain of the Lord, to the house of the God of Jacob; and he will teach us of his ways, and we will walk in his paths; for out of Zion shall go forth the law, and the word of the Lord from Jerusalem" (Isaiah 2:2-3). The *Jerusalem Bible* translation makes Isaiah's prophecy even more direct: "In the days to come *the mountain of the Temple of Jehovah* shall tower above the mountains and be lifted higher than the hills."[52]

An event of this magnitude and importance requires more than one witness. The Lord himself taught that "in the mouth of two or three witnesses every word may be established" (Matthew 18:16). To the prophecies of Isaiah and Brigham Young came a third witness—Elder Wilford Woodruff. In 1841, while in Boston, Elder Woodruff saw in vision that the Saints would come West. He also witnessed that "they built a temple and dedicated it."[53]

A few months later, Elder Erastus Snow and his companions were in Boston preaching the gospel in historic Boylston Hall. Caroline A. Joyce attended the meeting. She recalled:

> After the song a young man [Elder Snow] arose and took for his text these words: "And in the last days it shall come to pass that the Lord's House shall be established in the tops of the mountains and all nations shall flow unto it." He said the time for the fulfillment of this prophecy was near at hand; an angel had appeared unto a man named Joseph Smith, having the keys of the Everlasting Gospel to be preached to this generation, that those who obeyed it would gather out from the wicked, and prepare themselves for the coming of the Son of Man. . . . His words were like unto a song heard in my far off childhood, once forgotten but now returning afresh to my memory, and I cried for very joy.[54]

To the Tops of the Mountains

The "tops of the mountains" was the destination of the Saints, and they were going to need hundreds of wagons and thousands of cattle to transport supplies, tools, and personal belongings. Beginning on New Year's Day, 1845, the first of many meetings was held that led to the gradual transformation of Nauvoo into a major wagon manufacturing center. But where would they locate within those mountains? Brigham and his council, having read all they could find on the Rocky Mountains from government reports, trappers' journals, newspaper articles and maps, concluded that the area surrounding the Great Salt Lake was the most likely place to locate.[55] In March Brigham dreamed that he saw himself and Joseph searching for a place for the Saints when they came to a mountain that had several trails. Brigham located a trail that Joseph had overlooked, and was the first to arrive at the best location.[56]

LDS Church Historical Department.

Brigham's decision regarding the Great Salt Lake was ratified in open vision. Elder **George A. Smith** recalled, "After the death of Joseph Smith, when it seemed as if every trouble and calamity had come upon the Saints, Brigham Young . . . sought the Lord to know what they should do, and where they should lead the people for safety, and while they were fasting and praying daily on this subject, President Young had a vision of Joseph Smith, who showed him the mountain that we now call Ensign Peak, immediately north of Salt Lake City, and there . . . an ensign [flag] fell upon that peak, and Joseph said, 'Build under the point where the colors fall and you will prosper and have peace.'"[57]

With a temple to complete, supplies to gather, and many wagons to build, Brigham Young labored so hard that one day he received some wise counsel from across the veil. He wrote in his journal, "This morning I dreamed I saw Brother Joseph Smith, and as I was going about my business he says, 'Brother Brigham, don't be in a hurry. Brother Brigham, don't be in a hurry. Brother *Brigham, don't be in a hurry!*'"[58] Whether Brother Brigham heeded Joseph's admonition is unknown. Because of increasing mob violence, the exact destination of the Saints was kept a secret. When the Twelve publicly announced in September 1845 that they would soon leave for the West, Church leaders said they planned to settle on Vancouver Island. At other times they said that perhaps they would head for Oregon or Upper California. But whatever was stated, the Twelve knew that their exodus to the West would fulfill Biblical prophecy even beyond Isaiah's vision of the future temple. As Elder **Parley P. Pratt** bore witness to the Nauvoo Saints, "The Lord designs to lead us to a wider field of action. *This people are fast approaching that point which ancient prophets have long since pointed out as the destiny of the Saints of the last days.* We want a country where we shall have room to expand."[59]

LDS Church Historical Department.

Three Personages Lead the Way West

With the deaths of Joseph and Hyrum, it appeared evident that their role had ended in assisting the Saints to the West. **Amasa Lyman** learned that such was not the case. When the September 1845 public announcement from the Twelve made it essential for the Saints to leave Illinois as quickly as possible, Amasa Lyman had an experience that gave him great comfort. He wrote:

LDS Church Historical Department.

At the beginning of the last winter we spent in Illinois, about the time the last storm began to break upon us, we heard the thunders and threatenings of our enemies wherein they stated that we were to be driven away. At that time I was confined to my bed with sickness, but I heard the report of the proceedings day after day. . . . To get away was impossible at that time, and we knew that the longer we stayed the more we should be oppressed by our enemies.

After I had commenced to recover my health, one morning, while lying in my bed in open day, as wakeful as I am at this moment, the surrounding objects which I could see, all in an instant disappeared, and I found myself standing in a vacant lot in front of the Printing Office. I heard a rumbling noise. I turned round to look in the direction of Main Street, and behold! The whole country was filled with one moving mass of people that seemed to be traveling directly to the point where I stood. As they approached somewhat nearer, they seemed not to be traveling on the ground, but somewhat near the altitude of the tops of the buildings.

At the head of the company were three personages clothed with robes of white, something like those which many of us are acquainted with. Around [each] waist was a girdle of gold, and from this was suspended the scabbard of a sword—the sword being in the hand of the wearer. They took their places with their faces directly west; and as they stopped, the individual in advance turned and looked over his shoulder with a smile of recognition. It was Joseph; and the others were his two brothers, Hyrum and Don Carlos. To tell my feelings would be impossible. I leave you to guess them. After contemplating the scene a few moments, I was again in my bed as before, and the vision had disappeared. This was my assurance, in the commencement of our troubles there, that I received of the guardianship that was around us and the protection that we were receiving from the hosts of heaven."[60]

From Nauvoo to Winter Quarters

In October of 1845, Irene Hascall Pomeroy wrote to her father in Massachusetts from Nauvoo. Irene described some fascinating organizational plans for the Saints leaving Illinois for the West:

The church as a body intend[s] removing in the spring. . . . They have their arrangements made. They are going in companies consisting of one hundred families each, every company half a mile apart, every waggon two rods apart [thirty-three feet]. They make calculations for twenty-five hundred families. The rich [members] promise to sacrifice all except what they need themselves—to help the poor so all can go that wish. . . . You must come—how can I go and leave you on this side of the rocky mountains—and yet I cannot stay when God calls us to go. The twelve and Joseph received revelations concerning [the westward exodus] *before Joseph died.* We expect to go in the first company. . . .[61]

Brigham Young had initially planned for the Saints to leave Nauvoo in April 1846 and to travel directly from Illinois to the Rocky Mountains, but warnings and false rumors of Missouri mobbers and federal troops approaching from St. Louis were circulated, forcing the Mormons into leaving two months earlier. Their February departure subjected them to gale-force winds, torrential rain, snow, subfreezing temperatures, and axle-deep mud—not to mention that a large number of the Saints were poorly prepared for that epic journey. Many were city dwellers from the eastern United States and England, skilled in many crafts, but unaccustomed to feeding and harnessing the thousands of horses, oxen, and mules; milking cows; driving wagons; and herding other thousands of hogs, sheep, and livestock. And they were disorganized. Yet Brigham Young knew of the power of music to uplift the spirits and provide direction for people. Prior to leaving Nauvoo he had called upon the saints to go "with sweet instruments of music and melody and songs . . . for the time has come for the Saints to go up to the mountains of the Lord's house, and help to establish it upon the tops of the mountains."[62]

William Pitt's Nauvoo Brass Band provided enjoyable music for concerts and dances, but according to one source Brother Brigham was inspired to commission the writing of a hymn that would lift the spirit of *all* the Saints who would courageously cross the plains in wagon companies. Brigham's vanguard

LDS Church Historical Department.

company of pioneers had been on the trail for forty-three days and were encamped at Locust Creek, Iowa, on 15 April 1846. "I understand that when the pioneers were about to start across the trackless wilderness," said Heber J. Grant, "to go a thousand miles to a place they knew not where, a place that President Brigham Young had seen in vision, he said to Elder **William Clayton**, 'William, go and write a hymn that the Saints may sing at their camp fires, that shall be an inspiration and an encouragement to them in their journey across the plains,' and Brother Clayton withdrew and returned in a couple of hours with [the hymn]."[63]

Whatever the truth of that story, William needed inspiration that day, for he had spent the previous night on watch, attempting to head off horses and cattle that had been breaking into tents and wagons. He had the continual concern over the welfare of his pregnant plural wife Diantha, who had remained behind in Nauvoo with her parents. Then, that very day, came the news: Helen Kimball told William that Brother Pond had received a letter with the message that Diantha had delivered "a fine fat boy on the 30th," although she was ill with "ague and the mumps, all is well." Clayton chose the name Adriel Benoni Clayton for his new son (the child was later named, simply, "Moroni Clayton"), then sat down and composed "All is Well," now known as "Come, Come, Ye Saints."[64] The tune was drawn from a pamphlet entitled *Revival Melodies, or Songs of Zion,* published in Boston in 1842.

> "Come, come, ye Saints, no toil nor labor fear
> But with joy wend your way
> Tho' hard to you this journey may appear
> Grace shall be as your day."

"T'is better far for us to strive

Our useless cares from us to drive;

Do this, and joy your hearts will swell—

All is well! All is well!

. . . .

"We'll find the place *which God for us prepared,*

Far away in the West,

Where none shall come to hurt or make afraid;

There the Saints will be blessed.

We'll make the air with music ring,

Shout praises to our God and King;

Above the rest these words we'll tell—

All is well! All is well![65]

Utah State Historical Society.

The pioneers took 131 days to travel 300 miles across the state—an average of less than two-and-a-half miles of progress each day! Yet Providence occasionally smiled upon the weary travelers. **Jonathan Crosby** recalled that "during our first day's travel we came to a bad slue crossing in the road, and we got stuck fast so that we were compelled to unload in order to get out, but even then our team was not able to pull the empty wagon out. But just then, a large fine yoke of oxen came along the road behind us overtaking us, unattended by any person, and which we considered very providential aid. So I hitched them on the wagon with my own team, and pulled out easily. I then turned the strange oxen loose again, loaded in the things we had taken out, and traveled on. We looked upon that aid and help as being directly from our Heavenly Father."[66]

A Friendship Not Forgotten

LDS Church Historical Department.

While crossing Iowa, Joseph's close friend **Benjamin Johnson** received a spiritual affirmation of the Prophet's love for him at a time when he was most in need. Benjamin wrote:

I was sick . . . discouraged and almost hopeless, and under these influences dreamed I was alone in a strange place in a great concourse of strangers and enemies. I felt friendless and desolate, and sought to avoid notice by sitting down; and looking up, I saw a man come in with a broad-brimmed, white hat which partly covered his face. He sat down near me. I looked under his hat and saw it was the Prophet Joseph. I clasped him around the legs and wept for joy. He placed his mouth to my ear and told me to be comforted, that he was still my friend and would not forget me. My tears had not ceased, and when I awoke I was still crying for joy; and I felt from that hour a new inspiration that nothing else could have given me. It was to me, light in the midst of darkness, or like a lost happiness returned.[67]

Temporary Settlements in Iowa and Nebraska

Once Brigham Young reached the Missouri River he decided to establish Winter Quarters and several other temporary settlements on both sides of the river rather than continue west. There were compelling reasons for remaining: the season was late, supplies were short, the Saints were disorganized, many were ill, and five hundred of their ablest men had been recruited into the United States Army to take part in the Mexican War. Departing from Fort Leavenworth for San Diego, the Mormon Battalion would enter history as having completed the longest infantry march in American military history.

It was a rainy day on 15 July when members of the Twelve assembled in John Taylor's tent for a council meeting. Brigham Young told the brethren that "the next Temple would be built in the Rocky Mountains, and I should like the Twelve and the old brethren to live in the mountains, where the Temple would be erected, and where the brethren would have to repair to get their endowments."[68]

Two days later Elders Orson Hyde, Orson Pratt, and fifty wagons arrived in camp, and Elder Hyde wrote a report of the condition of the Saints in Nauvoo:

> While I remained at Nauvoo, I urged the brethren to get ready and start [for the West] as early as possible; and those who could not prepare to go on and overtake the first company to start and go as far as they could, and then stop in the Settlements in Iowa and go to work; and be sure and not wander off the main thoroughfare of the Saints, but remain on the track, and work to keep themselves, praying to God to help them, and watch for those who were passing that peradventure some one might pass with extra teams and hitch on to them and take them along, whereas if they should wander away from the main track such opportunities would escape their notice, and they still be left.
>
> Almon W. Babbitt, one of the Trustees of the Church, was very anxious that I should exert an influence to have the Saints stay in Nauvoo for his protection against the mob until he and his associates could settle up the business. I told him that I could not do it; and assured him that his safety was in his weakness, and not in his strength or numbers. Still, he would persevere to get me to use an influence to have a good many families remain in Nauvoo for the protection of the committee or trustees. *About this time an Angel of the Lord appeared to me in a night vision and spoke these words to me: "This people cannot stay here."*

The next day, a Mr. Edmonds, an attorney and a partner of Almon Babbitt, came to Elder Hyde "to persuade me to allow a large portion of the Saints in Nauvoo to remain there another season for protection. . . ." Elder Hyde recounted his reasoning with Almon Babbitt and testified that an angel said that the Saints must leave. "Mr. Edmonds," he said, "God being my helper I shall use all my influence and power at the conference and before it and after it, while I stay, to have all of the Saints follow their leaders as speedily as possible; and when I leave, I shall say to all the Saints behind, 'Come ahead as soon as possible and as far as you can, and then stop on the track.'"[69]

LDS Church Historical Department.

Almost four months later, as Brigham walked with several Church leaders along the bluffs of the Missouri River, he described his vision of Great Salt Lake Valley. It was important that those who presided over the Church had a clear understanding of their destination. **Willard Richards** wrote: "Fourteen Brethren climbed to the side of the bluff, where the President talked. He dreamed that he was on the top of the mountain. [He] walked a little way and saw Dr. Richards a few rods down the hill and said, 'I guess you can get along here.' [There] was a fine, smooth sand, and on the west, many beautiful hills, and barren, and valleys skirted with timber."[70] He also shared his experience with the presidents of the Seventies in his new home on Sunday two days later. He recorded in his journal, "I spoke to the Presidents and related a dream which I had concerning the Rocky Mountains."[71] Erastus Snow stated that "when President Young was questioned by any of the Pioneers as to the definite point of our destination, all he could say to them was, that he would know it when he should see it, and that we should continue to travel the way the Spirit of the Lord should direct us."[72]

Two Winter Quarters Visits from Joseph Smith

During the winter Brigham Young was in Winter Quarters before departing for the final leg of his journey, he had a visit from Joseph Smith in which the Prophet explained how the Saints' wagon trains should be organized. On 11 January 1847, Brigham wrote, "I told the brethren I dreamed of seeing Joseph, the Prophet, last night and conversing with him. . . . [We] conversed freely about the best manner of organizing companies for emigration, and so forth."[73] Three days later, on Thursday, 14 January, Brigham Young convened a council of Church leaders and gave them instruction. Later that day he wrote in his journal, "I commenced to give the Word and Will of God concerning the emigration of the Saints and those who journey with them." This revelation, now Section 136 of the Doctrine and Covenants, contains the now familiar and successful plan calling for captains to preside over each 100, 50, and 10 families. Did Joseph Smith unveil this plan in behalf of the Lord, or were there two revelations involved? We are unsure; Joseph may well have served as the Lord's spokesman on the matter.

Joseph paid Brigham a second Winter Quarters visit just one month later. Brother Brigham was ill and asleep about noon on 17 February when he dreamed that he spoke to Joseph, who was sitting in a chair.

> I . . . said to him: "Why is it that we cannot be together as we used to be, You have been from us a long time, and we want your society and I do not like to be separated from you." Joseph rising from his chair and looking at me with his usual, earnest, expressive and pleasing countenance replied, "It is all right." I said, "I do not like to be away from you." Joseph said, 'It is all right; we cannot be together yet; we shall be by and by; but you will have to do without me a while, and then we shall be together again."
>
> I then discovered there was a hand rail between us, Joseph stood by a window and to the southwest of him it was very light.

I was in the twilight and to the north of me it was very dark; I said, "Brother Joseph, the brethren you know well, better than I do; you raised them up, and brought the Priesthood to us . . . if you have a word of counsel for me I should be glad to receive it."

Joseph stepped toward me, and looking very earnestly, yet pleasantly said, "Tell the people to be humble and faithful, and be sure to keep the Spirit of the Lord and it will lead them right. Be careful and not turn away the small still voice; it will teach you what to do and where to go; it will yield the fruits of the Kingdom. Tell the brethren to keep their hearts open to conviction, so that when the Holy Ghost comes to them, their hearts will be ready to receive it. They can tell the Spirit of the Lord from all other spirits; it will whisper peace and joy to their souls; it will take malice, strife and all evil from their hearts; and their whole desire will be to do good, bring forth righteousness and build up the kingdom of God. Tell the brethren if they will follow the spirit of the Lord they will go right. Be sure to tell the people to keep the Spirit of the Lord; and if they will, they will find themselves just as they were organized by our Father in Heaven before they came into the world. Our Father in Heaven organized the human family, but they are all disorganized and in great confusion."

Joseph then showed me the pattern, how they were in the beginning. . . . I saw . . . where the Priesthood had been taken from the earth and how it must be joined together, so that there would be a perfect chain from Father Adam to his latest posterity. Joseph again said, "Tell the people to be sure to keep the Spirit of the Lord and follow it, and it will lead them just right." This counsel Joseph repeated three times, adding greater emphasis each time.[74]

A Flag Representing All Nations

One week after Joseph's second visit to Brigham Young, Brother Brigham said in council meeting that the time had come to prepare a flag that Joseph Smith had requested five days prior to his death. Joseph recorded, "I . . . gave orders that a standard [flag] be prepared *for the nations*."[75] Joseph was undoubtedly familiar with Isaiah's prophetic writings that stated: "And [the Lord] shall set up an ensign for the nations, and shall assemble the outcasts of Israel, and gather together the dispersed of Judah from the four corners of the earth" (KJV Isaiah 11:12). The flag was symbolic of the gathering of scattered Israel, and of all others from around the world, who would choose to become the Lord's covenant people.

After his assassination, Joseph Smith had shown such a flag to Brigham Young in vision—a flag that represented all nations. "I know where the spot is," Brigham had said to his council in Nauvoo, "and I know how to make this Flag. Joseph sent the colors and said where the colors settled there would be the spot [to settle]."[76] Later, on the Platte River, Brigham Young introduced this concept to his band of pioneers. He "spoke of the 'Standard' or 'Ensign' that would be reared in Zion to govern the Kingdom of God, and the nations of the earth, for every nation would bow the knee and every tongue confess that Jesus was the Christ. 'And this will be the Standard,' said Brigham, 'The Kingdom of God and His Law.' And on the Standard would be a flag of every nation under heaven come unto Zion."[77]

Now, in Winter Quarters, Brigham was ready to create the flag. He said that it should be prepared from the "best stuff in the Eastern markets." And he wanted it to be clearly seen: "What of a flag 16 feet by 8 feet on a mountain 5 miles off? I think 90 by 30 [feet] is better." President Young requested red, white, and blue fabric for the flag's field, with purple and scarlet for the insignia." Upon its completion, it was to fly from a mountain (perhaps Ensign Peak) rising above "a perfect Sea of Water" (no doubt the Great Salt Lake).[78] The flag, unfortunately, was never made, and the pattern does not now exist. There are clues that it may have been a variation of the American flag. For example, on 31 December 1846, Wilford Woodruff recorded this heartfelt plea in his journal: "I pray my Heavenly Father to lengthen out my days to behold the House of God stand upon the tops of the Mountains, and to see the Standard of Liberty reared up as an ensign to the nations to come unto to serve the Lord of Hosts."[79]

Camp of Israel

In Winter Quarters, five companies were designated and organized by Brigham Young for the trek across the plains in 1847. It is of interest that a typical American wagon train called itself a "train," and just as a railroad train, wagons—like passenger cars—could join on or be "uncoupled" from the train as they wished. The name "company" implies much more: careful organization, a common destination, and unity of purpose.

Brigham Young departed Winter Quarters for the West on 5 April 1847, leading a vanguard company of pioneers on what was to be a 111-day trek of 1,050 miles. Brigham named his 72-wagon company "Camp of Israel," for he considered the flight of the Saints from their enemies to be similar in spirit to the ancient Israelites who fled from bondage in Egypt. But consider what Brigham told his brother Joseph a month after leaving the beautiful "City of Joseph." "Nauvoo is no place for the Saints," Brigham said. "Do not think I hate to leave my house and home. No! Far from that. I am so free from bondage at this time, that Nauvoo looks like a prison to me. It looks pleasant ahead, but dark to look back."[80]

Daughters of Utah Pioneers Photo File.

First Brethren in the Valley

As the Saints neared Salt Lake Valley, Brigham Young sent **Orson Pratt** (left) and **Erastus Snow** (see photo, opposite page) ahead to scout out the best locations for plowing and planting. The two men arrived on 21 July with one horse between them. As the brethren first gazed upon the valley, they jubilantly cried out the sacred "Hosanna, Hosanna, Hosanna, to God and the Lamb!" for they knew that they had finally arrived at the Lord's designated place for the Saints. The next day Thomas Bullock saw the valley for the first time. He cried, "Hurra, hurra, hurra, there's my home at last!"[81]

LDS Church Historical Department.

This Is the Right Place!

Brigham Young, stricken with Rocky Mountain Spotted Fever, was in the rear of the company, which was divided into two sections. On 24 July, he was laying on a makeshift bed in Wilford Woodruff's carriage as it made its way down Emigration Canyon. Thirty-three years later Elder Woodruff, blessed with a photographic memory, recalled the events of that day. He told the Saints:

> On the 24th I drove my carriage, with President Young lying on a bed in it, into the open valley, the rest of the company following. When we came out of the canyon into full view of the valley, I turned the side of my carriage around, open to the west, and President Young arose from his bed and took a survey of the country. While gazing on the scene before us, he was enwrapped in vision for several minutes. *He had seen the valley before in vision, and upon this occasion he saw the future glory of Zion and of Israel, as they would be, planted in the valleys of these mountains.* When the vision had passed, he said: "It is enough. This is the right place. Drive on." So I drove to the encampment already formed by those who had come along in advance of us.[82]

Adaline Knight Belnap was a sister-in-law of Andrew Smith Gibbons, who was present in the encampment. Andrew told her, she said emphatically, that Brigham Young "was assisted out of the wagon by members of the party, and placing his cane on the ground he said three times, "This is the place; this is the place; this is the place.""[83]

Elder Erastus Snow recalled: "President Young said then, and afterwards to all the camp, that this was the place he had seen long since in vision; it was here he had seen the tent settling down from heaven and resting, and a voice said unto him, 'Here is the place where my people Israel shall pitch their tents.""[84]

LDS Church Historical Department.

Five years earlier, on 24 July 1875, Elder Snow gave a similar account to the Saints gathered in the **St. George Tabernacle**. Charles L. Walker wrote that "Pres. E. Snow . . . show[ed] that the Lord had guided his servant Brigham all the way across the trackless plains and deserts. Said that Pres Young told the Saints that as soon as he saw the place he should know it. Said that as soon as Br Brigham entered the Valley of the Great Salt Lake he saw the sign from the Lord of Hosts, for Israel to stop. The Tent that had appeared above them before, now came down and rested on the ground."[85] Brigham Young himself explained, "The Spirit of light rested on me and hovered over the valley, and I felt that there the Saints would find protection and safety. This is the place where I, in vision, saw the Ark of the Lord resting."[86]

Brigham Young saw a parallel between the Saints fleeing the United States and the Israelites fleeing Egypt. He named his wagon company "Camp of Israel." When the ancient Israelites established a base camp in the wilderness, the first thing they erected was the portable tabernacle, which protected the sacred Ark of the Covenant. Then the twelve tribes pitched their tents facing the four sides of the walls which surrounded the tabernacle. Here in the Rocky Mountains the Saints were to erect a temple, and the city was to face that temple on all four sides.

The Brethren Visit Ensign Peak

Brigham Young's portion of the pioneer company arrived on Saturday, 24 July. Sunday they spent in worship at their base camp, now known as Washington Square and the home of Salt Lake City's City and County Building. Monday morning, Brigham Young pointed his finger toward a sugar-loaf shaped hill to the north and said, "I want to go there." The brethren rode on their horses about two-thirds of the way, then hiked up a relatively short but steep incline the rest of the way. Wilford Woodruff wrote, "We went north of the camp about five miles, and we all went on to the top of a high peak in the edge of the mountain, which we considered a good place to raise an ensign."[87]

Utah State Historical Society.

Wilford was the first to reach the summit. He observed, "Brigham Young was very weary in climbing to the peak, he being feeble [from the effects of mountain fever]." After surveying the scene, Brigham then told the assembled men, 'This is Ensign Peak. Now, Brethren, organize your exploring parties, so as to be safe from Indians; go and explore where you will, and you will come back every time and say this is the best place."[88]

Ensign Peak was the very peak Joseph Smith had shown Brigham Young in vision. Since no flag was present to symbolically fulfill Isaiah's prophecy, Heber C. Kimball said, "We will sometime raise an ensign here!" The brethren formed a circle while Heber brought forth a yellow bandanna covered with black

spots. He tied the bandanna to **Willard Richards'** walking cane and held it above them as the brethren were united in thanksgiving.[89]

Two poems, later set to music, commemorated this signal event. Parley P. Pratt penned:

See on yonder distant mountain
Zion's standard wide unfurled,
Far above Missouri's fountain.
Lo! it waves for all the world.
Freedom, peace and full salvation
Are the blessings guaranteed,
Liberty to every nation,
Every tongue, and every creed.
Come, ye Christian sects and pagan,
Pope, and Protestant, and Priest,
Worshipers of God or Dagon,
Come ye to fair freedom's feast.
Come, ye sons of doubt and wonder,
Indian, Moslem, Greek, or Jew,
All your shackles burst asunder,
Freedom's banner waves for you.
Cease to butcher one another,
Join the Covenant of peace,
Be to all a friend, a brother,
This will bring the world release.
Lo! Our King! the great Messiah,
Prince of Peace, shall come to reign;
Sound again, ye heavenly choir,
Peace on earth, good will to men.[90]

Five years after the visit of the brethren to Ensign Peak, pioneer **Joel Hills Johnson** wrote "Deseret," later known as "High on the Mountain Top," descriptive of Ensign Peak's symbolic significance. Johnson was well familiar with Isaiah's visions of the gathering of Israel in the last days. Although he was ill and needed to rest, he said that he felt an overwhelming urge to write—the impulse, he said, seemed like "fire in my bones." He wrote:

Daughters of Utah Pioneers Photo File.

> High on the mountain top a banner is unfurled.
> Ye nations, now look up; it waves to all the world.
> In Deseret's sweet, peaceful land,
> On Zion's mount behold it stand!
>
> For God remembers still his promise made of old
> That he on Zion's hill Truth's standard would unfold!
> Her light should there attract the gaze
> Of all the world in latter days.[91]

The Prophet Isaiah prophesied: "And [the Lord] will lift up an ensign to the nations from far, and will [signal] to them from the end of the earth: and, behold, they shall come with speed swiftly; none shall be weary nor stumble among them" (Isaiah 5:26-27; see also 2 Nephi 15:26-27). Isaiah also proclaimed: "And [the Lord] shall set up an ensign to the nations, and shall assemble the outcasts of Israel . . . from the four quarters of the earth" (Isaiah 11:12; see also 2 Nephi 21:12).

Why does the Lord desire to gather the tribes of Israel together in the last days? Joel Hills Johnson wrote:

His House shall there be reared, his glory to display,
And people shall be heard in distant lands to say:
We'll now go up and serve the Lord,
Obey his truth and learn his word.
For there we shall be taught the law that will go forth,
With truth and wisdom fraught, to govern all the earth.
Forever there his ways we'll tread,
And save ourselves with all our dead.[92]

LDS Church Historical Department.

Isaiah prophesied that in the latter days, a temple would be built in the tops of the mountains: "And it shall come to pass in the last days, that the mountain of the Lord's house shall be established in the top of the mountains, and shall be exalted above the hills; and all nations shall flow unto it " (Isaiah 2:2-3).

In his epic *Comprehensive History of the Church,* Elder **Brigham H. Roberts** wrote the following:

"The Ensign" that these Latter-day Saint Pioneers had in mind, and of which they had frequently spoken en route, was something larger and greater than any national flag whatsoever; and what it was meant to represent was greater than any earthly kingdom's interest. . . . This "Ensign" . . . concerned not one nation, but all nations; not one epoch or age, but all epochs and all ages; not nationality but humanity, is its scope and concern. It was the sign and ensign of the Empire of the Christ; it was a prophecy of the time to come when the kingdoms of this world would become "the kingdoms of our Lord, and of his Christ; and he shall reign forever and forever."[93]

The Temple Site Seen in Vision

Two days later, **Brigham** walked between two branches of City Creek, planted his cane into the ground, and said, "Here we will build the Temple of our God." Ground would not be broken until 14 February 1853; the cornerstones were laid on 6 April. Brigham Young said, "Five years ago last July I stood not ten feet from where we have laid the chief cornerstone. I have not inquired what kind of a temple we should build. Why? Because I saw it in vision before me. I never look upon that site but what I see the temple before me."[94]

LDS Church Historical Department.

Daughters of Utah Pioneers Photo File.

That evening, the pioneers made camp on the site. **Levi Jackman** wrote in his journal: "July 28th. This evening Brother Young called the camp together and the men that had been exploring made their report. They had found no place that looks so well as this place. Many of the brethren expressed their feelings and all seem to feel that this was the place to stop. Brother Young then said he wanted to know how the brethren felt in regard to it. *But he knew that this was the place for the city, for he had seen it before,* and that we were now standing on the southeast corner of the temple block. A vote was taken then on the subject and all voted that this be the place to stop."[95] As **Orson Pratt** began his survey for Great Salt Lake City in August,

LDS Church Historical Department.

his starting point was the southeast corner of the future Temple Square, southeast being symbolic of the greatest source of light and truth.

According to James Brown, Brigham Young prophetically declared:

> God has shown me, that this is the spot to locate His people, and here is where they will prosper; He will temper the elements to the good of the Saints; He will rebuke the frost and the sterility of the soil, and the land shall become fruitful. . . . We shall build a city and a temple to the Most High God in this place. We will extend our settlements to the east and west, to the north and to the south, and we will build towns and cities by the hundreds, and thousands of the Saints will gather in from the nations of the earth. This will become a great highway of the nation. Kings and emperors and the noble and wise of the earth will visit us here. . . .[96]

Within a month, Brigham Young and other leaders began the long trek back to Winter Quarters to prepare their families to come to Great Salt Lake Valley. On 24 November 1847, President Young wrote to Nathaniel Felt: "The whisperings of the Spirit is now to all saints, 'gather yourselves together, to the place which has been pointed out, for a place of rest & Salvation; a place for the building of the House of the Lord, a place "sought out," and a city which need not be forsaken [if] the inhabitants thereof will work righteousness.'"[97]

The Designated Place of Gathering

The Rocky Mountains were now the designated place of gathering for the Latter-day Saints from throughout the world. They would prove to be a mixed lot. During his mortal ministry, the Lord explained that his missionary "fishermen" sometimes caught "fish" seemingly of varying worth (see Matthew 13:47-

48); of such, he taught, is the kingdom of God. Not long after the California gold rush began, many of the Utah Saints left to pursue mineral wealth. "It seemed as though the whole community would be carried away with the spirit of gold," Brigham recalled, "which caused much anxiety in my mind and enlightened my understanding." The Prophet Joseph eased Brother Brigham's anxieties. He came in the dreams of the night and instructed Brigham about the worth of souls, comparing them to sheep and goats. Said Brigham,

> I dreamed I was a little north of the hot springs [a mile north of Great Salt Lake City] with many of my brethren. . . . I . . . stood there some time talking with the brethren, when I looked up towards the road on my right, and behold I saw brother Joseph . . . riding on a waggon [with] a tent and other camping implements . . . as though he had been on a journey of some length. He alighted from the waggon, and came to where we were standing. I looked, and saw, following the waggon, an almost innumerable flock of sheep of all kinds, sizes, colours, and descriptions, from the largest, finest sheep I ever saw, down to the ugly decrepit dwarf. The wool on the large ones, I thought, was as white as snow; then the next smaller ones had also nice fine wool on them, and some were black and white; others had coarse long wool upon them, approximating hair; and so on, until they became a mixture of goats and sheep.
>
> I looked on the strange flock and wondered. While I was looking, I asked Joseph what in the world he was going to do with such a flock of sheep, and said to him, "Why, brother Joseph, you have the most singular flock of sheep I ever saw: what are you going to do with them?" He looked up and smiled, as he did when he was living, and as though he was in reality with me, and said, "They are all good in their place."

"So it is with this people," said Brother Brigham. "If you can only find a place for the goats, they answer the end for which they were made."[98] The Lord would need everyone to create Zion out of a near-barren wilderness. Although the site was designated for the house of the Lord, six years would pass before ground would be broken, and forty-six years would pass before that sacred structure was completed and dedicated.

First "Temple" in Deseret

LDS Church Historical Department.

In the meantime, other sites were employed for the performance of sacred temple ordinances. During October Conference of 1849, **Addison Pratt** (left), **James Brown** (below), and Hiram H. Blackwell were called to serve as missionaries in the Society Islands (Tahiti) in the South Pacific. Addison was also called to preside over the Church in the islands.

Daughters of Utah Pioneers Photo File.

Brown and Blackwell had received their endowments in Nauvoo, but not Pratt, he having been away on a mission to the South Pacific at the time.

In Nauvoo, Joseph Smith explained that under certain circumstances mountain peaks could be used for temple ordinances on occasion, much as Moses on Mount Sinai.[99] Ensign Peak was so designated by Brigham Young. Addison Pratt arose early Saturday morning, 21 July, and hiked atop Ensign Peak, accompanied by Brigham Young and nine brethren. The peak was consecrated, and a three-hour sacred ceremony was conducted to endow Addison.[100] Afterward, Pratt was blessed by the assembled brethren in behalf of his mission.

Council House (right), a two-story adobe structure, was erected on the corner of South Temple and Main streets in 1850. It was the first public building erected in the territory. On the second floor, the temple rooms were temporarily dedicated for temple

work. **Brigham Young's office** (below left) was used from time to time, until the **Endowment House** (below right) was built on the

northwest corner of Temple Block. Erected in 1855, it was used by the Saints for baptisms for the dead, and endowments and sealings for the living until the Salt Lake Temple was nearly completed.

Led By the Spirit to Come West!

The first official July 24th celebration, led by Elder Lorenzo Snow, was held just three days after Addison Pratt's sacred Ensign Peak experience. During the day, Brother Brigham affirmed the divine revelation behind the selection of the Great Basin for the Saints. He said: "Joseph Smith and myself had both seen this place years ago, and that is why we are here."[101] The work of gathering to the West had begun in earnest. Yet personal dreams and revelation that led people to join the Church and emigrate to Great Salt Lake Valley did not cease.

Annie Hicks

Seventeen-year-old Annie Hicks was one such person. Annie was born in Barking, Essex, England, to parents who belonged to the Church of England. She wrote:

> I was alone, or rather away from my own people at the time I first heard the gospel, and I think I loved it the first time I heard it; it seemed so quiet and pleasant to me. I embraced the Gospel and was baptized on January 17, 1855 in the White Chapel Branch, in London, England.
>
> Shortly after my baptism, before I had been confirmed my relatives sent me a terrible book against the Mormons, marking it in may places for me to read. The tales were so wicked, I was afraid I had done wrong and decided to ask the Lord to direct me aright, never doubting that I would be answered. I fervently pleaded with our Father to answer my prayer that night as my confirmation was to take place the following morning.
>
> I immediately was comforted by a wonderful dream. A large book, the Book of Life, was opened before me and the leaves were turned in rapid succession until the page with my record was found. A loud, clear voice spoke to me saying, "This is the way; walk ye in it." I was overjoyed at this revelation and have never doubted the Gospel from that time on. You may be assured I was confirmed the next day.
>
> From then on my relatives were unkind and cruel to me. I worked very hard to obtain enough money to come to America. I would knit from early morning until evening in the London workshop. On the 25th of May, 1856 I sailed for America on the ship *Horizon,* beginning my journey to Zion. I crossed the plains in the belated handcart company of *Edward Martin.* We underwent numerous hardships and lost many of our good and faithful band on the way.

Annie, alone, found work doing "knitting, sewing and embroidery" for the Ellerbeck family. One year later she married

Absalom Pennington Free, a patriarch, and bore seven children. She remained active and faithful for the rest of her life.[102]

David John

About the time Annie was working in London to earn ship's passage money, **David John**, a Welshman, received a powerful revelation that changed his life forever. David was born in Pembrokeshire, Wales, in 1833, into a family that boasted many Baptist ministers among their ancestors and relatives. David's parents were determined that he should train for the ministry, but when David was fifteen he heard the message of the gospel and was baptized in 1847. His parents were so enraged at his baptism that he finally agreed to attend a theological college until he was of age. When he was about nineteen, David enrolled in a Baptist college in the town of Haverford West, and spent the next four years preparing to be a preacher.

David's life changed forever when, toward the end of January 1856, he had a most remarkable dream. He wrote:

> I dreamt that I saw an angel of the Lord. After he had talked a little with me, he placed his right hand on my left shoulder. His eyes were of a dark brown color, but full of glory. His voice was clear, but full of power and authority. While in his presence I beheld very high mountains. He told me that they were the *everlasting hills,* over or by which the Latter-day Saints were going to their gathering place. "'Why," said he, "are you spending your time in vain here? How is it you will not join the Church of Christ and spend your time there?" I replied, "I hope I am in the Church now, am I not?" "You

know better," he said. "Do not ask questions that you know perfectly well, but go on unto perfection. Look towards the firmament [heavens]." I looked and beheld the air full with people of every sect and party. There I saw Christ sitting upon His throne in great glory, and the people gathered themselves before Him to be judged. Those that had pleased Him, He commanded to stand on His right hand, and those that did not, on His left. He judged them one by one, till they composed two straight lines, running parallel one against the other for the distance of about one mile. Those on the left were those of the different sects and parties of the day; and those on the right were Latter-day Saints. The Saints seemed lovely, and all smiled, looking in the face of Jesus as one man looks on another. But the other line seemed miserable, and full of discontent, sorrow and grief, turning their faces from Jesus, and could not abide His presence.

"According to this vision," I said, "the Saints are right, but the others are not." "You see," he answered, "who is right and who is wrong. Look," said he, "on thy right hand." I looked, and there beheld *a large and very extensive valley—the most beautiful land I ever saw.* We were standing on one side of it, which was flat. On the side we stood, were high and beautiful trees. Under the shadow of one of them we stood from the heat of the sun, which was very powerful. On the other side were mountains or hills, but not very high. Those extended to the extremity of the valley. The beauty and glory of the valley . . . was beyond description. "Oh, my God," I exclaimed, "I never knew that such a beautiful scene as this belonged to our earth." "This," said the angel, "shall be thy inheritance and thy seed after thee forever, if thou wilt obey the commandments of God and do right in the flesh."

"Look, behold thee," said he. I then found myself in a large and beautiful building. There I saw on the stand one that I knew [probably Orson Pratt], preaching the principles of life. "This," said my guide, "is the house of the Lord."

At this I awoke, believing that the spirit of the Lord and angels filled the room. I arose and bowed myself before God in prayer, and desired Him, if that messenger was from Him, to make it known to me once more by the same messenger; if not, to hide the vision from me. I again retired to rest, and soon fell into a deep sleep, when suddenly the same personage appeared, and made known unto me some of the same thing; but he rebuked me this time for spending my time where I was. He also said: "Thou wert foreordained before the foundation of the world to come forth in this age to assist to build the Kingdom of God upon the earth, and now the time is up. If thou wilt obey the commandments of God, thy days shall be long on the earth; if not, thy days shall be short, says the Lord!"

John spent the rest of the night in "deep reflection." The next morning he was excused from his studies, his teacher believing him to be unwell. Visiting the home of a Mormon missionary, he obtained several books and pamphlets and renewed his knowledge of the restored Church. Now twenty-three years of age, he told his parents, his teacher, and fellow students of his decision to become a Latter-day Saint once more. John was rebaptized on 6 February 1856. He labored in various capacities as a missionary for five years, when he was released to emigrate to Utah. In the West he served in several positions of responsibility before being set apart as president of the Utah Stake in 1901. His dream or vision had been fulfilled to the letter.[103]

LDS Church Historical Department.

Hard Times Make Solid Saints

Brigham Young's own visions impelled him to action, to bring about the destiny of the Saints as much as it lay in his power to do so. In 1856 this practical man declared, "I have Zion in my view constantly. We are not going to wait for angels, or for Enoch and his company to come and build up Zion, but we are going to build it."[104]

By 1865, thousands of Saints had arrived in the territory. Great Salt Lake City was a beautiful community, and many other settlements were emerging from the wilderness soil. Brigham reflected on the experiences of the past, saying:

> My soul feels hallelujah; it exults in God, that He has planted this people in a place that is not desired by the wicked; for if the wicked come here they do not wish to stay, no matter how well they are treated, and I thank the Lord for it; and I want hard times so that every person that does not wish to stay for the sake of his religion will leave. This is a good place to make Saints, and it is a good place for Saints to live; *it is the place that the Lord has appointed, and we will stay here, until He tells us to go somewhere else.*[105]

The Beginning of the Final Act

In his classic work, *The World and the Prophets,* Hugh Nibley wrote: "The entrance of the Saints into Salt Lake Valley was one of the great moments in world history. *It was that moment at which the assembly upon the hills and the mountains began at a place which the Lord had appointed from the beginning.* It was the beginning of the final act of what we know as world history. It was a vindication of prophets ancient and modern. It was a day of days to be remembered."[106]

Brief Biographies

Information in this section was drawn in part from *Membership of The Church of Jesus Christ of Latter-day Saints: 1830-1848*, compiled by Susan Easton Black, Provo, Utah: Religious Studies Center, BYU, 1989.

Thomas Bullock was born 23 December 1816, in Leek, Staffordshire, England, the son of Thomas and Mary Hall Bullock. Thomas was baptized 20 November 1840 in Leek. He married Henrietta Rushton and two plural wives, who bore him twenty-five children. He served as a secretary for Joseph Smith, recording over 700 pages of Church history. He was clerk for the Brigham Young wagon company; chief clerk for the Utah Territorial House of Representatives; chief clerk, Historian's Office; clerk of probate court and country recorder for Summit County, Territory of Utah. He died in Coalville, Summit County, Utah, 10 February 1885.

Anson Call was born 13 May 1810, in Fletcher, Franklin County, Vermont, the son of Cyrill and Sally Tiffany Call. He was baptized 21 May 1834 in Kirtland, Ohio. He married Mary Flint and five plural wives. Anson assisted in the colonization of several settlements in Utah. He was a merchant, farmer, and probate judge.

Diantha Farr Clayton was born 12 October 1828, in Charleston, Orleans County, Vermont, the daughter of Winslow and Olive Hovey Freeman Farr. Her family joined the Church and later became members of the Nauvoo 4th Ward. Diantha became a plural wife of William Clayton on 26 January 1846.

Jonathan Crosby, Jr., was born 20 July 1807, in Wendell, Franklin County, Massachusetts, the son of Jonathan and Lois Barnes Crosby. He was baptized 2 December 1833. Jonathan married Caroline Barnes 25 October 1834. A musician, he played the bass viol in his youth and offered vocal instruction in the Kirtland Temple. He traveled to Missouri in Kirtland Camp. A cabinetmaker by trade, he labored on Joseph Smith's Kirtland home, the Kirtland Temple, and the Nauvoo Temple. He died 12 June 1892 in Beaver, Beaver County, Utah Territory.

Jonathan Dunham was a member of Kirtland Camp and a colonel in the Nauvoo Legion. He served missions to New York and Indiana. Jonathan died in 1846.

Stephen Martindale Farnsworth was born 8 October 1809, in Dorset, Bennington County, Vermont, the son of Reuben and Lucinda Kent Farnsworth. He married Julia Ann Clark and two plural wives. Stephen was baptized in 1840. A farmer, he died 19 September 1885, in Tuba, Coconino County, Arizona.

Annie Hicks Free was the fifth wife of Absolom Pennington Free. She bore seven children.

Stephen Hezekiah Goddard was born 23 August 1810, in Champlain, Clinton County, New York, a son of Stephen G. and Sylvia Smith Goddard. He was baptized 27 February 1836. Stephen married "Alamantha," Lucinda Vaugn, and Mary Ann Lewis. He served as a warden for the University of the City of Nauvoo, and as a trustee for the Nauvoo Concert Hall. Stephen was also a skilled builder and mason. Active in music circles, he led a choir that serenaded the Prophet Joseph Smith at the Mansion House one New Year's Eve. Known as the most handsome man in his company, he served as a captain of ten when the vanguard pioneers left Winter Quarters for the West in 1847. In Great Salt Lake City he led the first choir in the Old Tabernacle, and later served as the second director of the Tabernacle Choir. Against the counsel of Brigham Young, he traveled to California to make his fortune and was unsuccessful. He eventually became the senior member of the 27th Quorum of Seventy. In his later years, suffering from ill health, he lived with a daughter in California, returning to Salt Lake City in 1897 for the Jubilee celebration of the pioneers. He died on 10 September 1898 in San Bernardino, California.

Mosiah Lyman Hancock was born 9 April 1834, in Kirtland, Geauga County, Ohio, the son of Levi Ward and Clarissa Reed Hancock. He was baptized 10 April 1842. Mosiah married Margaret McCleve and four plural wives. He lived in Nauvoo, Illinois; Great Salt Lake City, Salt Lake County; Harrisburg, Washington County; Manti, Sanpete County; and Orderville, Kane County; Territory of Utah; and Taylor, Apache County, Arizona. In Utah he explored the Green River. He also served a mission among the Moqui and Navajo Indians. A carpenter, he died 14 January 1909, in Hubbard, Apache County, Arizona.

Joseph Holbrook was born 16 January 1806, in Florence, Oneida County, New York, the son of Moses and Hannah Morton Holbrook. He was baptized 6 January 1833. Joseph was married to Nancy Lampson and six other wives, who bore him at least nineteen children. He marched in Zion's Camp. Joseph was later wounded during the Battle of Crooked River in Missouri. He helped construct the Kirtland and Nauvoo temples. He was a member of the Nauvoo Legion, and was a special policeman in Nauvoo. Joseph came west in 1848. He was a probate judge and city recorder in Davis County. He died 14 November 1885, in Bountiful, Davis County, Utah.

Oliver Boardman Huntington was born 14 October 1823, in Watertown, Jefferson County, New York, the son of William and Zina Baker Huntington. He was baptized 7 October 1836 in Missouri. He married Mary Melissa Neal and three plural wives. He lived in Missouri; Grantsville, Tooele County; Provo and Springville, Utah County; and St. George, Washington County,

Territory of Utah. A schoolteacher, Master Mason, bee inspector, school trustee, farmer and stock raiser, Oliver gathered reminiscences and folk tales about Joseph Smith and about events in early Church history. He labored on the Nauvoo Temple, a mission to England, explored a route to Carson Valley; and was a missionary to the Indians. He died on 7 February 1907, in Springville, Utah County, Utah.

Levi Jackman was born 28 July 1797, in Vershire, Orange County, Vermont, the son of Moses French and Elizabeth Carr Jackman. He was baptized 7 May 1831, in Portage County, Ohio. Levi married Angeline Myers on 13 November 1817. He later married Sally Plumb, Lucinda Harmon, Mary Vale Morse, Delia Byam, Elizabeth Davies, Caroline Christiansen, and Ruth Rodgers. Levi lived in Kirtland, Geauga County, Ohio; Clay County and Caldwell County, Missouri; Great Salt Lake City, Salt Lake County; and Pondtown (Salem), Utah County. He marched with Zion's Camp in 1834 and was a member of the Clay County high council; a justice of the peace in Far West, Caldwell County, Missouri; a missionary in 1844; and a wagon maker in Nauvoo. Levi labored on the Kirtland and Nauvoo temples. He was one of the original pioneers who arrived in Utah in 1847. Levi served on the first high council in Great Salt Lake City and was later ordained a patriarch. He was a saddle tree maker and farmer. He died 23 July 1876, in Salem, Utah County, Utah.

David John was born 29 January 1833 in Pembrokeshire, Wales, the son of Daniel and Mary Williams John. David came from a long line of Baptist ministers. His parents decided that their son would study for the ministry. He was baptized a Latter-day Saint on 6 February 1846 at the age of 13, but he had to bear constant persecution until he agreed to stay apart from the Church until he was of age. At age 23 he was attending a Baptist college in ministerial training, when he had a visitation from an angel that led him to be rebaptized. He married Mary Wride and Jane Cree, who bore him twenty children. David served a mission in Wales. He lived in Great Salt Lake City and Provo, Territory of Utah. In Provo he served as superintendent of the Sunday School Association and later, the Deseret Sunday School Union. He was called to be mission president of the Welsh Mission. David was a counselor and later president of Utah Stake. He was on the first board of directors of Brigham Young Academy. He died 24 December 1908 in Provo, Utah.

Benjamin Franklin Johnson was born 28 July 1818, in Pomfret, Chautaqua County, New York, the son of Ezekiel and Julia Hills Johnson. He was baptized in 1835. He was married to Melissa Bloomfield LeBaron and six other women. He lived in Kirtland, Geauga County, Ohio; Adam-ondi-Ahman, Missouri; Nauvoo County, Hancock County, Illinois; Bonaparte, Iowa; Salt Lake City, Payson, Santaquin, Spring Lake, and Scootempah (Rock Lake), Utah; Mesa, Maricopa County, Arizona; and Mexico. Benjamin made brick for the Kirtland Temple. A close friend of the Prophet Joseph Smith, Benjamin managed the Nauvoo Mansion Hotel. He crossed the plains to Utah in 1848. He served in the legislature of Deseret, then was called to settle Summit Creek (Santaquin) and Scootempah. He served a mission in Hawaii. He was a bishop in Spring Lake. He also served as a patriarch. He was vice-president of the United Order in Santaquin. He wrote "My Life's Review." He died 18 November 1905, Mesa, Maricopa County, Arizona.

Joel Hills Johnson was born 23 March 1802, in Grafton, Worcester County, Massachusetts, a son of Ezekiel and Julia Hills Johnson. He was baptized 1 June 1831. Joel married Anna Pixley and four other wives and fathered twenty-nine children. Joel lived in Kentucky, New York, Ohio, Illinois, and Utah. An inventor, he patented the shingle cutter machine. He was a farmer, stockraiser, justice of the peace, and legislator. Joel came to Utah in 1848. During his life he served as a missionary, bishop, stake president, high counselor, and patriarch. Joel composed songs and hymns. He died 24 September 1882, at Johnson, Kane County, Utah.

Amasa Mason Lyman was born 30 March 1813, at Lyman, Grafton County, New Hampshire, a son of Roswell and Martha Mason Lyman. He was baptized in 1832 and served missions in Ohio and Virginia, New York, northern Illinois and Wisconsin, Tennessee and southern Illinois, and Mississippi. He was a member of Zion's Camp. Amasa served as a member of the First Quorum of Seventy and was ordained an apostle 20 August 1842 by Brigham Young. He married Louisa Maria Tanner and eight other women and fathered thirty-seven children. He came west with Brigham Young in 1847, and was called in 1850 to help colonize a site in southern California (now San Bernardino). In 1862 he colonized Fillmore, Utah. In 1867 he was dropped from the Twelve for preaching false doctrine, including the denial of Christ's divinity. He embraced spiritualism, was excommunicated 12 May 1870, and died 4 February 1877 in Fillmore. He was buried in a black suit and boots. Twenty-one years later, Martha Lyman Roper, a daughter, experienced a manifestation in which Amasa called for help. She desired to embrace him, but found that a great chasm separated them. He said that he was tired of his black clothes, and asked that she enlist the help of his son Francis Marion Lyman, an apostle, to help him so that he could be with his family "whom he loved and longed for." Elder Lyman likewise had seen his father in a dream "and pled his cause." In 1908 President Joseph F. Smith, by proxy, restored "all . . . former blessings, authority and power" to Amasa.

Father McBride was a youth in Kirtland, Geauga County, Ohio, where he heard Joseph Smith relate the story of the First Vision. Little else is known of his life, except that he lived in St. George, Utah, where he served as a patriarch.

Hopkins "Hop" Carl Pender was born 7 October 1824, in Knoxville, Tennessee. He was baptized in Illinois in 1839. Hop married Mary Janet "Jeanette" Drake in Iowa. They moved to Utah, residing in the Thirteenth Ward. During the early days the Penders experienced many trials, including fighting crickets and eating roots to survive. A popular "fiddler," Hop played for dances at the Social Hall and other settings. Sent by Brigham Young to help colonize Las Vegas, Hop and the other settlers were severely beaten by Indians, who stripped clothing from their bodies, and stole or burned their property. Later, he served as sheriff of Weber County. Returning to Salt Lake City to live, Pender faithfully attended Sunday afternoon services at the Tabernacle "on the front bench to the left of the aisle, directly in front of the stand." He was known as an extremely sensitive man. Toward the end of his life he lived in the Seventeenth Ward. He died in 1910, at age 89, and buried in the Salt Lake Cemetery on 5 April.

Paulina Eliza (or Elizabeth) Phelps was born 20 March 1827, at Tazewell, Illinois, a daughter of Morris Charles and Laura Clark Phelps. She married Amasa Mason Lyman and was mother of seven children. She died 11 October 1912, at Parowan, Iron County, Utah.

William Wines Phelps was born 17 February 1792, at Hanover, Morris County, New Jersey, a son of Enon and Mehitable Goldsmith Phelps. William was baptized 27 August 1835, in Kirtland, Ohio. He was excommunicated 10 March 1838, and was rebaptized 11 December 1845, in Nauvoo, Illinois. He married Stella Waterman and five other women, and was father of at least eleven children. He lived in New Jersey; Kirtland and Dayton, Ohio; Liberty, Clay County, and Far West, Caldwell County, Missouri; Nauvoo, Illinois; and Salt Lake City, Utah. William was a printer, justice of the peace, newspaper editor, and warden. Joseph Smith received Doctrine & Covenants 55 regard-

ing Phelps' mission. William was the Church's first printer, printing the Evening and Morning Star newspaper, as well as the Book
of Commandments. He served as a missionary and was a counselor in the Presidency of the Church in Missouri. He wrote
many hymns. Phelps came west in 1848. He died 6 March 1878,
in Salt Lake City, Utah.

Addison Pratt was born 21 February 1802, at Winchester,
Cheshire County, New Hampshire, a son of Henry and Rebecca
Jewell Pratt. He was baptized in May or June 1837. He married
Louisa Barnes, who bore him four children. Addison served two
missions to the Society Islands (Tahiti) as mission president. He
later became disaffected from the Church and followed the
Spiritualist movement. Addison died 14 October 1872,
Anaheim, Orange County, California.

Parley Parker Pratt was born 12 April 1807, at Burlington,
Otsego County, New York, a son of Jared and Charity Dickinson
Pratt. He was a brother of Orson Pratt. Parley was baptized 1
September 1830, at Seneca Lake, New York, by Hyrum Smith.
He married Thankful Halsey and eleven other women, and
fathered at least thirty children. Parley was a missionary in the
United States, Canada, Europe, and Chile. The seventh ordained
apostle in the Restored Church, Parley authored many Church
pamphlets. In Utah he served on the territorial legislative council and as a regent of the University of Deseret. He also helped to
develop the Deseret Alphabet. He died at the hands of an assassin 13 May 1857, in Van Buren, Crawford County, Arkansas.

Mariah (Maria) Pulsipher was born 15 June 1822, in
Susquehanna, Broome County, New York, the daughter of Zera
and Mary Ann Brown Pulsipher. She was baptized 11 January
1832. Mariah married William Burgess, Jr., near Lima, Adams
County, Illinois, 17 September 1840. She bore nine children.
She lived in Kirtland, Geauga County, Ohio; Adam-ondi-

Ahman, Missouri; Lima, Adams, and Nauvoo, Hancock County, Illinois; and Huntington, Emery County, Utah. She died 17 March 1893, in Huntington, Emery County, Utah.

Samuel Whitney Richards was born 9 August 1824, in Richmond, Berkshire County, Massachusetts, the son of Phinehas and Wealthy Dewey Richards. He was a brother of Franklin D. Richards. He was baptized on 14 October 1838. He married Mary Parker and four other women, and fathered at least twenty-eight children. Samuel lived in Nauvoo, Illinois, and Great Salt Lake City, Utah Territory. He was a carpenter on the Nauvoo Temple. He served twice as a missionary in the eastern United States, and later as president of the Eastern States Mission. He also served in Illinois, Canada, and Great Britain, and was later a mission president of the British and European missions. Sixteen years of his life were spent on missions. He was a sergeant in the Nauvoo Legion, and served both in Nauvoo and Salt Lake City. Samuel came to Utah in 1849. He was a farmer, city councilor, alderman, and police judge, and a school trustee and regent of the University of Deseret, which he helped to construct. He was U.S. commissioner of Davis County, Salt Lake County justice, and member of the territorial legislature. Samuel wrote poems and songs. A patriarch, he died 26 November 1909, in Salt Lake City, Utah.

Willard Richards was born 24 June 1804, in Hopkinton, Middlesex County, Massachusetts, the son of Joseph and Rhoda Howe Richards. He was baptized 31 December 1836, in Kirtland, Geauga County, Ohio, by Brigham Young, a cousin. He was a doctor in Massachusetts. Willard served as first counselor to Joseph Fielding Smith in the British Mission. Willard was married to Jennetta Richards and three other wives, and fathered at least seven children. He served as a Nauvoo city council member, Joseph Smith's secretary, and general Church clerk. He was present in Carthage Jail when Joseph and Hyrum Smith

were assassinated. He came west where he served as second counselor of Brigham Young. He served as secretary of the provisional
government of the State of Deseret and of the Territory of Utah.
Willard served as postmaster in 1850. He was Church Historian
and Recorder. He founded the Deseret News and was its first editor. He lived in Kirtland, Geauga County, Ohio; Warsaw and
Nauvoo, Hancock County, Illinois, and Great Salt Lake City,
Salt Lake County, Utah. He died 11 March 1854, in Great Salt
Lake City, Utah.

Bathsheba Wilson Bigler Smith was born 3 May 1822 on a 300-
acre plantation in Shinnston, Harrison County, West Virginia, a
daughter of Mark and Susanna Ogden Bigler. She and her family were baptized in 1837 and moved to Nauvoo, Illinois, two
years later. She married Elder George A. Smith in 1841. She was
a talented portrait painter and served in many positions of leadership. She was the fourth general president of the Relief Society.
A matron of the Salt Lake Temple, she also officiated in the
Nauvoo, Logan, Manti, and St. George temples. A member of
the board of directors of the Deseret Hospital, she promoted
nurses' training. She helped win the right of women to vote in
Utah. Bathsheba died 20 September 1910 in Salt Lake City.

Eliza Roxcy Snow Smith was born 21 January 1804 in Becket,
Massachusetts, the daughter of Oliver and Rosetta Pettibone
Snow and sister of Lorenzo Snow. Her family moved to Mantua,
Ohio, where she became a follower of the teachings of Alexander
Campbell and Sidney Rigdon. In 1835 she was baptized as a
Latter-day Saint. Eliza afterward lived with Joseph and Emma
Smith in Kirtland and Nauvoo, and taught their children. She was
blessed with the gift of tongues, which she used throughout her
life. In 1842 her constitution for a women's benevolent society led
to the Prophet Joseph Smith's organization of the Relief Society.
Eliza served as its first secretary, and was later its second president.
She was a plural wife of Joseph Smith. Called by Brigham Young,

she served as Nauvoo Temple recorder and matron of the Salt Lake Endowment House. Under his direction she founded the Young Ladies' Retrenchment Association, now known as the Young Women. Inspired by Aurelia Spencer Rogers, she advocated the adoption of the Primary Association, which was approved by President John Taylor. She was known as "Zion's Poetess" for her many poems. She wrote nine books and also composed several noted hymns, including "O My Father." Eliza died at the Lion House in Salt Lake City on 5 December 1887.

George Albert Smith was born 26 June 1817 in Potsdam, New York, the son of John and Clarissa Lyman Smith. His father was a brother to Joseph Smith, Sr. A religious youth, he was a Congregationalist until he became a Latter-day Saint through his testimony of the Book of Mormon. Large in stature as a youth, he became a bodyguard for Joseph Smith. He served seven missions in a nine-year period, preaching the gospel in the American Midwest, South, North, and East, and in England. Called to the apostleship in 1839, he came west with the first pioneer company in 1847. He served in the territorial legislature, helped settle the community of Parowan, and was commanding military officer during two Indian wars in southern Utah. He replaced Willard Richards as Church Historian, and completed Joseph Smith's unfinished History of the Church. In 1861 he joined other Church leaders to establish the "Dixie Mission," which was to raise cotton, among other products. The mission was successful but ultimately unprofitable. The city of St. George is said to have been named in his honor. Seven years later he served as first counselor to Brigham Young. He was noted for his weight, his humor, and hundreds of brief but excellent sermons delivered in a "deep rolling voice." He died at age 58 on 1 September 1875 of "lung disease."

Joseph Fielding Smith, Sr. was born 13 November 1838 in Far West, Caldwell County, Missouri, the son of Hyrum and Mary

Fielding Smith. He never forgot his mother's intense grief when she learned of the assassination of his father and uncle in Carthage Jail. At age nine he drove a team of oxen and otherwise helped his mother to move from Winter Quarters to Great Salt Lake City in 1848. At his mother's death in 1852, he and his sister Martha were enrolled in a Sugarhouse school by their uncle George A. Smith. Joseph was expelled for defending Martha from physical punishment by the teacher. He was ordained an elder and sent to the Sandwich Islands (Hawaii) as a missionary at age fifteen. He was released four years later at age nineteen. He later served three missions to Great Britain, another mission to Hawaii, and a mission with Orson Pratt to collect historical information in the Midwest. He married six women. In 1866 he was ordained an apostle. He served as a counselor to Brigham Young, John Taylor, Wilford Woodruff, and Lorenzo Snow. He also served as a councilman in Salt Lake City and Provo, a member of the territorial legislature, and member of the Utah Constitutional Convention. In 1901 he became the sixth President of the Church, serving for seventeen years. Under his direction, historic properties in Vermont, New York, Missouri, and Illinois were purchased. Also, the Church Administration Building, Hotel Utah, Bishop's Building, and Deseret Gymnasium were erected, and temples announced for Hawaii and Alberta. He approved the seminary program, Scouting, and the Family Home Evening program for the Church. He became the first prophet to visit Europe. He prophesied that temples would dot Europe one day. Prior to his death he received the "Vision of the Redemption of the Dead," now canonized as Doctrine & Covenants 138. He died of pneumonia on 19 November 1918 in Salt Lake City.

Erastus Fairbanks Snow was born 9 November 1818 in Saint Johnsbury, Vermont, the son of Levi and Lucina Streeter Snow. He was distantly related to Lorenzo Snow. Converted and baptized in 1832, Erastus served as a missionary in Ohio,

Pennsylvania County, New Jersey, Maryland, and Massachusetts, and was one of the first missionaries in Denmark. He married Artimesia Beaman and three other wives, and fathered thirty-five children. He came to Utah with Brigham Young's company, and was the first Latter-day Saint, with Orson Pratt, to enter Salt Lake Valley. Two years later he became the first man ordained an apostle after the death of Joseph Smith. In 1854 he became the presiding officer of the Church in St. Louis, and he published the Luminary, a periodical that defended the Church and its doctrines. In 1861 he presided over the "Cotton Mission" in southern Utah with Orson Pratt. He was called upon by President John Taylor to locate sites in Mexico and the American border for Mormon colonies. He died on 27 May 1888, age sixty-nine, in Great Salt Lake City, Territory of Utah.

William Carter Staines was born 26 September 1818 at Higham Ferrers, Northampton, England, the son of William and Blanche Potter Staines. As a child he disliked school but loved horticulture and floriculture, and enjoyed working in his father's garden. When he was thirteen he fell on ice and suffered a spinal deformity that caused him to be short in stature. Ten years later he was converted and baptized. He was blessed with the spiritual gifts of healing, prophecy, speaking in unknown tongues and their interpretation, all of which was fulfilled during his lifetime. In 1843, while William was aboard the ship "Swanton" en route for America, he had a vision of the Prophet Joseph Smith, which enabled him to instantly recognize the Prophet upon his arrival in Nauvoo. After Joseph and Hyrum Smith were martyred at Carthage Jail, William witnessed Brigham Young as he spoke "with a voice like the voice of the Prophet Joseph Smith" at the time that Sidney Rigdon was presenting his claim he be the "guardian of the Church." Staines came to Utah in 1847. He married Lillias Thompson Lyon in Salt Lake City. He later became an agent for Brigham Young. Staines died at Great Salt Lake City, Territory of Utah, in 1881.

Wilford Woodruff was born 1 March 1807 in Farmington, Hartford County, Connecticut. As a youth he learned the trade of miller. Religious, he spent much time in prayer and reading the scriptures. In Richland, New York, he was baptized on 31 December 1833. Within four months he marched with Zion's Camp to Missouri. He later served missions to Arkansas and Tennessee, the Eastern States and Fox Islands, and Great Britain, baptizing hundreds of people. He was ordained an apostle 26 April 1839 by Brigham Young. He later served as President of the European and Eastern States missions. He was married to Phoebe W. Carter and seven other women. He fathered thirty-three children. He kept many volumes of journals which are valuable for understanding early Church history and doctrine. He served as Church historian for thirty-three years. In Nauvoo he was a member of the city council and Nauvoo Legion. Elder Woodruff came West with the first pioneer company in 1847. He served in the territorial legislature for twenty-two years, and was president of the Deseret Agricultural and Manufacturing Society. He loved farming, and sought to improve species of plants and trees. He was a noted fisherman. He served as the first president of the St. George Temple, and was baptized for the signers of the Declaration of Independence and other famous individuals. On 7 April 1889 he was sustained as fourth president of the Church. On 25 September 1890 he issued the Manifesto, which forbade future plural marriages. On 6 April 1893 he dedicated the Salt Lake Temple. One year later he organized the Genealogical Society of Utah. In 1896 he and his counselors issued a "political manifesto," explaining that men holding prominent positions of Church leadership should either be released or receive permission to run for public office to avoid neglecting their calling. He died at age ninety-one in San Francisco on 2 September 1898.

Brigham Young was born 1 June 1801 in Whitingham, Vermont, the son of John and Abigail (Nabby) Howe Young. He lived on a series of farms and learned hard work. Although he only received eleven days of education, he became a skilled carpenter, joiner, painter, and glazier. He was educated in religious principles by his mother. He married Miriam Works, who bore two daughters. A Methodist, he was converted to the Church through the Book of Mormon. Baptized on 14 April 1832, he was a missionary in Canada and marched in Zion's Camp before being called as one of the first apostles on 14 February 1835. He served a mission to England, and was in the East promoting Joseph Smith as a candidate for the presidency of the United States when Joseph and Hyrum Smith were assassinated. Upon returning to Nauvoo, he defended the right of the apostles to preside over the Church in response to Sidney Rigdon's desires for authority. He would later be sustained as the second President of the Church. He supervised the completion of the Nauvoo Temple, and assisted in endowing over five thousand Saints. He led the vanguard company of pioneers to the Great Basin, where he directed the settlement of over four hundred communities and assisted thousands of Latter-day Saints to emigrate to Utah through the Perpetual Emigrating Fund. President Millard Fillmore appointed him governor of the territory and superintendent of Indian affairs. Sixteen of his wives bore him fifty-six children. He broke ground for the Salt Lake Temple, and authorized sites in Logan and Manti, Utah. He died on 29 August 1877 in Great Salt Lake City, Utah Territory.

Lorenzo Dow Young was born 19 October 1897 at Smyrna, Chenango County, New York, the son of John and Abigail Howe Young. He was a brother of Brigham Young. Lorenzo was baptized in 1831. He married Persis Goodall and four other wives and fathered at least seventeen children. He learned the trade of blacksmith. Lorenzo hauled the first stone for the Kirtland Temple. He lived in Kirtland, Daviess County, Missouri, and Nauvoo, Illinois. He was a member of the first pioneer company to leave Winter Quarters for the West. Lorenzo grew the first garden flowers and wheat in Salt Lake Valley. He served as bishop of the Eighteenth Ward. He also served as a patriarch. He died 21 November 1895.

Notes

All who undertake a serious study of the westward movement of the Latter-day Saints owe a debt to Hyrum L. Andrus, "Joseph Smith and the West," *Brigham Young University Studies,* vol. 21 (Spring-Summer 1960), no. 2; Lewis Clark Christian, "A Study of Mormon Foreknowledge of the American Far West Prior to the Exodus (1830-February 1846)," master's thesis, Brigham Young University, 1972; and Ronald K. Esplin, "A Place Prepared": Joseph, Brigham and the Quest for Promised Refuge in the West," May 1982, for their excellent scholarship on this subject.

1. B.H. Roberts, *The Life of John Taylor, Third President of The Church of Jesus Christ of Latter-day Saints,* Salt Lake City: George Q. Cannon and Sons Co., 1892, p. 96.

2. See, for example, Brigham Young, *Journal of Discourses,* 10:316 (Liverpool: Asa Calkin, 1858; hereafter referred to as *JD*), (July 17, 1864),; *JD,* 12:93-94 (June 30, 1867); Joseph F. Smith, *JD,* 24:250-54 (August 19, 1883); Erastus Snow, *JD,* 25:101-103 (9 March 1884); Martha Thomas, quoted in *Daniel Thomas Family History,* pp. 33-34 (1927); Seymour B. Young, *General Conference Addresses,* October 1899, p. 57.

3. Brigham Young, *Journal History,* entry for 15 March 1857, The Church of Jesus Christ of Latter-day Saints Historical Department, Library Division, p. 1. (Hereafter referred to as LDS Church Historical Department.)

4. Photocopy of a signed affidavit by Paulina Elizabeth Phelps Lyman, witnessed on 31 July 1903 by James Jack, notary.

5. *History of Joseph Holbrook 1806-1885, written by his own hand,* Mabel F. Holbrook and Ward C. Holbrook, ed., 1977, n.p., pp. 22-24; emphasis and some punctuation added.

6. *The Evening and Morning Star,* vol. 1, no. 5 (October 1832), n.p.

7. *Millennial Star,* vol. 54 (1892), p. 605; *Conference Reports,* 8 April 1898, p. 57.

8. Lorenzo Dow Young, *Fragments of Experience,* sixth book of the Faith Promoting Series, Salt Lake City: Juvenile Instructor Office, 1881, pp. 42-45.

9. Joseph Smith, Jr., *Documentary History of the Church of Jesus Christ of Latter-day Saints* 2:381, Salt Lake City: Deseret Book Co., eighth printing, 1974. (Hereafter referred to as HC.)

10. *Autobiography of Erastus Snow,* typescript, dictated to his son, Franklin R. Snow, Brigham Young University, Harold B. Lee Library, Special Collections. (Hereafter referred to as BYU Library, Special Collections.)

11. Brigham Young, *JD,* 3:209 (17 February 1856); emphasis added.

12. "Biographical Sketch of the Life of Luman Andros Shurtliff," as quoted in Duane S. Crowther, *The Prophecies of Joseph Smith,* Salt Lake City; Bookcraft, 1963, p. 366.

13. Heber C. Kimball, *President Heber C. Kimball's Journal,* Salt Lake City, Juvenile Instructor, 1882, p. 77.

14. *Oliver Boardman Huntington Diary, Written by Himself, 1878-1900,* BYU Library, Special Collections, n.d., p. 204.

15. Bishop Burdick wrote a letter of inquiry to Joseph Smith as a result of Jonathan Dunham's statements. See Thomas Burdick letter, 28 August 1840, Joseph Smith Collection, Church Historical Department, Archives Division, as quoted in Ronald

K. Esplin, "'A Place Prepared': Joseph, Brigham, and the Quest for Promised Refuge in the West," paper, May 1982, p. 3.

16. Wilford Woodruff, L. John Nuttall Papers, Container #4, Letter Press Book #4, BYU Library, Special Collections, p. 285.

17. *HC,* 5:85-86.

18. Autobiography of Anson Call, BYU, Harold B. Lee Library, Special Collections, pp. 6-7, 18-20. See also Edward W. Tullidge, *History of Northern Utah and Southern Idaho,* Biographical Supplement, pp. 271-272, as quoted in "Joseph Smith and the West," by Hyrum Andrus, *BYU Studies,* Spring/Summer 1960, p. 134-35; emphasis added.

19. Elder Claudius V. Spencer, "Recollections of the Prophet," Memorial Services, Sixteenth Ward Meeting House, Sunday Evening, 23 December 1894, as quoted in Brian Stuy, ed., *Collected Discourses* (1896-1898), vol. 5, Woodland Hills, Utah: B.H.S. Publishing, 1992, p. 35.

20. Brigham Young, *JD,* 11:16 (11 December 1864).

21. Orson Pratt, 26 April 1846, *John D. Lee Diary,* and a letter written by Lyman Wight to Wilford Woodruff, 24 August, 1857, as quoted in Duane S. Crowther, *The Prophecies of Joseph Smith,* Salt Lake City: Bookcraft, 1963, p. 366.

22. Lewis Clark Christian, "A Study of Mormon Foreknowledge of the American Far West prior to the Exodus (1830-February 1846)," Master's thesis, Brigham Young University, 1972 , p. 67.

23. *Joseph Smith Diary,* entry for 20 February 1844, in *HC* 6:222.

24. B. H. Roberts, *Comprehensive History of the Church of Jesus*

Christ of Latter-day Saints, 6:223-27, Salt Lake City: Deseret News Press, 1930. (Hereafter referred to as CHC.)

25. "Reminiscences of Bathsheba W. Smith," *Young Woman's Journal* 16 (1905) p. 549

26. Samuel Whitney Richards, *CR,* October 1905, pp. 87-89. An apparent earlier draft was written upon note paper imprinted with "Shoshone, Idaho, _____ 190__." On page 4, Richards wrote:

> "Upon hearing this the first response of my soul was, I am not the one wanted, and I will decline at once, but as I was about to offer my resignation a voice whispered to me "Wait! no hasty action;" with which I complied. I went home and retired for the night, after first pleading most earnestly with the Lord to let me know what I should do in this matter which seemed to me the most important of my life.

> "I retired to my bed, and during the 4 hours of my sleep, my prayer was more than answered, and in the morning I was prepared to continue my relation with the company, and prepare the outfit required for the journey. I performed the journey in my sleep, and had shown to me important events to transpire, and the condition of the Earth itself, to its complete restoration of its Eden beauty and grandeur, as when man was first placed upon it in a state of innocence and immortality to which all must come in the restoration of all things spoken of by Prophets and holy men since the world began."

Extracts from a holograph account of the dream in the possession of Rama Richards Buchanan, Salt Lake City, Utah.

27. *Mosiah Hancock Autobiography,* typescript, BYU Library, Special Collections, pp. 28-29.

28. This story has been incorrectly attributed to George Goddard since 1946, when E. Cecil McGavin, gave George credit in his book *Nauvoo the Beautiful,* SLC: Stevens and Wallis, 1946, p. 127. However, Stephen H. Goddard related the story to George Goddard, hence the confusion. See *Journal History,* entry for 26 July 1897, LDS Church Historical Department, Library Division.

29. *Oliver Boardman Huntington Diary,* entry for 27 September 1897, p. 425.

30. As quoted in *Diary of Charles Lowell Walker,* vol. 2, Logan: Utah State University Press, 1980, pp. 524-25.

31. *Wilford Woodruff Journal,* vol. 2 (1 January 1841 - 31 December 1845), Midvale, Utah: Signature Book, 1983, p. 449. See entry for February 25, 1844.

32. Benjamin F. Johnson letter to George F. Gibbs, 1903, in E. Dale LeBaron, "Benjamin Franklin Johnson: Colonizer, Public Servant, and Church Leader," Master's thesis, Brigham Young University, 1967, pp. 332-33.

33. William C. Staines entry, "Early LDS Membership Data," LDS Collectors Library, Orem, Utah: Infobases International Inc., 1995, pp. 18-19.

34. *Allen Stout Journal,* typescript, Brigham Young University, Harold B. Lee Library, Special Collections, p. 20.

35. Mariah Pulsipher, "Autobiography," in Kenneth Glyn Hales, ed., *Windows: A Mormon Family,* Tucson, Arizona: Skyline Printing, 1985, p. 181. Orem, Utah: Infobases International Inc., ibid.

36. *Autobiography of Parley P. Pratt,* Salt Lake City: Deseret Book Co., 1970, p. 333; emphasis added.

37. Helen Mar Whitney, "Scenes in Nauvoo After the Martyrdom of the Prophet and Patriarch," *Woman's Exponent* 11 (1 February 1883), p. 130.

38. Quoted in Matthias Cowley, *Wilford Woodruff, His Life and Labors,* SLC: Deseret News, 1909, p. 234. See journal entry for 22 October 1844.

39. *Wilford Woodruff Journal,* vol. 2, entry for 25 February 1844, p. 449; *The Deseret Weekly,* vol. 53, p. 642.

40. Joseph F. Smith, as quoted in Brian Stuy, *Collected Discourses,* vol. 5, entry for 23 December 1894, p. 27.

41. As quoted in *The Private Journal of William Hyde,* n.p.: William Layne Woolf, publisher, n.d., p. 15. BYU Library, Special Collections.

42. *The Life and Record of Anson Call, commenced in 1839,* n.p.: Ethan L. Call and Christine Shaffer Call, publishers, 1987, p. 29.

43. Andrew Jenson, *Latter-day Saint Biographical Encyclopedia,* vol. 1 (1901-1936). Salt Lake City: Andrew Jenson History Company, 1901, p. 695.

44. William Clayton Journal, entry for 16 July 1845, as quoted in George D. Smith, ed., *An Intimate Chronicle: The Journals of William Clayton,* Salt Lake City: Signature Books, 1991, pp. 173-75.

45. *Wilford Woodruff's Journal,* vol.1, 19 August 1844, p. 449.

46. *Brigham Young Diary,* entry for 24 January 1845, as quoted in Esplin, "A Place Prepared," p. 15. See also Leonard J. Arrington, *Brigham Young: American Moses,* New York: Alfred A. Knopf, 1985, p. 119.

47. Stephen M. Farnsworth, "A Vision," LDS Church Historical Department, Archives Division. See also *Journal of Samuel Pitchforth,* typescript, entry for 8 February 1857, pp. 4-5, in possession of the author.

48. Brigham Young, *HC,* 7:567 (12 Jan 1846).

49. Brigham Young, *HC,* 7:561 (2 January 1846); emphasis added.

50. Ibid.

51. *John D. Lee Diary,* entry for 13 January 1846, as quoted in D. Michael Quinn, "The Flag of the Kingdom of God," The Historian's Corner, *Brigham Young University Studies,* vol. 14, no. 1 (Autumn, 1973), p. 105.

52. Isaiah 2:1. *The Jerusalem Bible,* Garden City, New York: Doubleday and Co., Inc., 1966, p. 1144; emphasis added.

53. L. John Nuttall Papers, Container #4, Letter Press Book #4, BYU Library, Special Collections, p. 285.

54. August Joyce Crocheron, *Representative Women of Deseret,* Salt Lake City: J.C. Graham & Co., 1844, pp. 99-101, as quoted in Carol Lynn Pearson, comp., *Daughters of Light,* Salt Lake City: Bookcraft, Inc., 1977, p. 51.

55. See Orson Pratt's statement as recorded in *Norton Jacobs Diary,* 23 July 1847, BYU Library, Special Collections.

56. *Seventies Book B,* minutes, entry for 9 March 1845. LDS Church Historical Archives Division.

57. George Albert Smith, *JD,* 13:85-86 (20 June 1869).

58. Brigham Young, *HC,* 7:435 (17 August 1845).

59. Parley P. Pratt, sermon given 6 October 1845, quoted in James R. Clark, *Messages of the First Presidency,* 1:283-84, Salt Lake City: Bookcraft, Inc., 1965.

60. Amasa Lyman, *JD* 5:58-60 (19 July 1857).

61. Letter of Irene Azula Hascall Pomeroy, Nauvoo, Illinois, October 1845, to Captain Ashbell Green Hascall, North New Salem, Franklin County, Massachusetts, as found in *"Letters of Irene B. Hascall Pomeroy* to her parents and relatives in North New Salem, Massachusetts, covering the period: May 1845-August 1841." Microfilm collection, Utah State Historical Society Library, Salt Lake City, Utah. Emphasis, creation of sentences, and some capitalization and punctuation has been added.

62. Brigham Young, quoted in Clark, *Messages of the First Presidency,* 1:333.

63. Heber J. Grant, *Conference Reports,* October 1919, p. 3.

64. James B. Allen, *Trials of Discipleship: The Story of William Clayton, a Mormon,* Urbana: University of Illinois Press, 1987, p. 202, p. 218 n. 27.

65. William Clayton, "Come, Come, Ye Saints," *Hymns of The Church of Jesus Christ of Latter-day Saints* (Salt Lake City: The Church of Jesus Christ of Latter-day Saints, 1985), no. 30.

66. *Jonathan Crosby Autobiography,* Utah State Historical Society, p. 29.

67. Benjamin F. Johnson, *My Life's Review,* Independence, Missouri: Zion's Printing & Publishing Company, p. 120.

68. Watson, *Manuscript History of Brigham Young,* entry for 15 July 1846, p. 241.

69. Ibid., pp. 187-88; emphasis added.

70. *Journal of Willard Richards,* entry for 6 November 1846, LDS Church Historical Department, Archives.

71. Watson, *Manuscript History of Brigham Young,* entry for 8 November 1846, p. 445.

72. Erastus Snow, as quoted in *The Utah Pioneers: Celebration of the Entrance of the Pioneers into Great Salt Lake Valley.* Thirty-Third Anniversary, 25 July 1880. Salt Lake City: Deseret News Printing and Publishing Establishment, 1880, p. 44.

73. Watson, *Manuscript History of Brigham Young,* entry for 11 January 1847, p. 501-502.

74. *HC,* 6:528-30 (23 February 1847).

75. *HC,* 6:528 (22 July 1844); emphasis added.

76. See *John D. Lee Diary,* entry for 13 January 1846, *BYU Studies,* p. 106.

77. *HC,* 3:276 (29 May 1846).

78. Winter Quarters Council Meeting minutes, entry for 26

February 1847, Brigham Young Papers, LDS Church Historical Department, Archives Division.

79. *Wilford Woodruff Journal,* appendix to the entry for 31 December 1846, p. 107.

80. Watson, *Manuscript History of Brigham Young,* entry for 9 March 1846, p. 75.

81. *Thomas Bullock Diary,* entry for 22 July 1847, LDS Church Historical Department, Archives Division, as referred to by Esplin, "A Place Prepared," ftnt. 122

82. *Wilford Woodruff,* as quoted in *Utah Pioneers,* p. 23.

83. *An Autobiography of Gilbert Belnap,* typescript, LDS Church Historical Department, Archives Division.

84. Erastus Snow, as quoted in *Utah Pioneers,* p. 47.

85. A. Karl Larson, *Diary of Charles Lowell Walker,* vol. 1, Logan, Utah: Utah State University Press, 1980, p. 412 . Some correction of punctuation.

86. Roberts, *CHC,* 3:223-24. Some punctuation added for clarity.

87. *Wilford Woodruff Journal,* entry for Monday, 26 July 1847, p. 236.

88. As quoted by George A. Smith, *JD,* 13:86 (20 June 1869).

89. Ronald N. Walker, "A Banner Is Unfurled": Mormonism's Ensign Peak," *Dialogue: A Journal of Mormon Thought,* vol. 26, no. 4 (Winter 1993), p. 81.

90. Parley P. Pratt, Church Hymnal, Hymn no. 92, p. 102, as quoted by Charles W. Penrose, *Conference Reports,* October 1919, p. 48.

91. Joel Hills Johnson, "High on the Mountain Top," *Hymns of The Church of Jesus Christ of Latter-day Saints,* no. 5.

92. Ibid.

93. B. H. Roberts, *CHC,* 3:275.

94. Brigham Young, *JD,* 1:132 (6 April 1853).

95. *Levi Jackman Journal,* typescript entry for 28 July 1847, BYU Library, p. 41; emphasis added.

96. *Autobiography of James Brown,* pp. 119-23, LDS Church Historical Department, Archives Division. Punctuation and capitalization added.

97. *Brigham Young Papers,* LDS Church Historical Department, Archives Division.

98. Brigham Young, *JD,* 6:320-2l (April 7, 1852).

99. Roberts, *CHC,* 3:386-87.

100. Jenson, *Latter-day Saint Biographical Encyclopedia,* vol. 3, pp. 698-99.

101. *Miscellaneous Minutes,* 22 July 1849, as quoted in Esplin, "A Place Prepared," p. 33.

102. "Grandma Free," *Our Pioneer Heritage,* Salt Lake City: Daughters of the Utah Pioneers, 1961, p. 184.

103. Jenson, *Latter-day Saint Biographical Encyclopedia,* vol. 1, pp. 489-91.

104. Nibley, *Approaching Zion,* Salt Lake City: Deseret Book Co., 1989, p. 32; emphasis added.

105. Ibid., emphasis added.

106. Hugh Nibley, *The World and the Prophets,* Salt Lake City: Deseret Book Co., 1962, p. 217; emphasis added.